WATER GARDENS

Simple Projects, Contemporary Designs

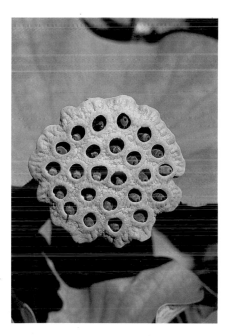

A GARDEN DESIGN BOOK

WATER GARDENS

Simple Projects, Contemporary Designs

HAZEL WHITE

Photography by Matthew Plut

CHRONICLE BOOKS
SAN FRANCISCO

Dedicated to:

My sisters and brothers (HW)

Stan and Yolanda (MP)

Library of Congress
Cataloging-in-Publication Data:
White, Hazel.
Water gardens: simple projects, contemporary
designs / by Hazel White; photography by
Matthew Plut
p. cm.
"A garden design book."
Includes bibliographical references (p.) and index.
ISBN 0-8118-1406-8 (pb)
1. Water gardens—Design and construction.
2. Garden Structures—Design and construction.
3. Water in landscape architecture.
I. title.
SB423.W48 1998
635.9'674—dc21 97-6981
CIP

Printed in Hong Kong.

Designed and typeset by David Bullen Design.

Distributed in Canada by Raincoast Books
8680 Cambie Street
Vancouver, British Columbia V6P 6M9

10 9 8 7 6 5 4 3 2 1

Chronicle Books
85 Second Street
San Francisco, California 94105

Web Site: www.chronbooks.com

CONTENTS

INTRODUCTION

I once had a postcard of Winston Churchill sitting with his broad tweed-covered back to the camera, looking out to a pond set between rolling lawns in the foreground and a long view of misty green downs. His head was tilted toward the water in contemplation, his shoulders comfortably slumped and the lines of them curved in the same natural arc as the shore of the pond and the tops of the downs. In that low place, where his gaze had drifted and stayed, the water had drawn light from the pearl gray sky down to the ground, splitting the mild landscape open with a deep pool of brightness. A shadow was stealing across the water, recording the coming of a rain shower and the drawing in of the day.

Water, whether it's in a bucket or a bowl or a fountain or even a drainage ditch, establishes a sure focal point to a landscape. We are drawn to it outdoors in the same way that we are drawn toward an open fire indoors. Close to water, even more than at the edge of a grand view or under a canopy of ancient trees, a stillness creeps over us, and we feel our relation to the elements and the rest of the natural world. Plants grow particularly tall and green in the splash zone; butterflies bathe in the mud. When it's quiet, animals come to drink, birds to fish.

Still water is gently ornamental. Small events flicker across the surface. Cold blue-black swirls bob like oil on a pond before the sun rises, then beams of rose and gold sunlight clip the crests of the waves. Shards of ice too thin to hold float in a bucket in fall, followed by a scoop of weightless snow. The water skin in a ditch catches debris from the seasons—fall leaves and seed cases, spring blossoms and pollen, summer dust. In the clear channels float reflections of mists, storm clouds building, moons, bird migrations, satellites passing over at night, the undersides of lotus and taro leaves, the new blue window frames.

Moving water—in fountains and springs—generates action, sound, and cheer in a sunny part of a garden. Water flies through the air or pours out of a bank, chuckling, slapping its way downward, pushed on by a constant renewing from the source. Waves rock against fountain basins, form soft black puddles on bank ledges, the light spinning in the currents. If the basin walls are high or the spring enfolded in foliage, the sound is magnified, and the drips plop loudly into the pool, as if in a grotto.

At my grandmother's house in England, a farmhouse called Shute, water ran continuously out of a drainpipe set in a very high bank close to the side of the house. The wall was mildewed with dampness, the window on that side so overshadowed by the bank that little light came into the kitchen, but the light was a reassurance that the earth hadn't slid up to and buried the house. Water from the chute washed over the garden, down the slope, spreading wider and moving more slowly until some of it puddled at the gate of the bull yard and the rest seeped into the pond.

The pond was lined with duck feathers and droppings and algaed pebbles on one side. If it didn't rain, the water would clear and the alders on the far bank would be mirrored in the black water below. Under the alders grew clumps of primroses and violets, which were always in flower on Mother's Day, but we couldn't reach them. The ducks paddled along that bank though and tipped themselves tails up into the silty black water.

Part of the fascination of water gardens is the watery world under the surface we can't know. Algae often spread through the water in spring, feeding off the water nutrients. If you let the algae be, some may turn into emerald slime, soft as silk. It's a daredevil pleasure to immerse a hand into the bottomless-looking water and rake the algae threads off the lily stems and from under the lily leaves. Aquatic plant roots thrive in pots of mud down in the gloom, furred over with silt like shipwrecks; stems with flower buds on their ends weave up through the dark water to the light between the leaves. Fish help us imagine what it might be like to live in a watery world; our eyes follow them into the shadows, around rocks, nosing up roots from a pot.

Water gardens come in various sizes, with various combinations of features. Even a small deck has space for more than one. To catch and hold up the view of the weather in the sky each day, or to record a maple tree turning from green to scarlet and purple, a garden needs one bowl with a super-generous rim, and the water fresh and brimming to the top. A second container, on a pedestal so that the water is close enough to touch, might hold a pattern of water clover leaves. In a large garden, there may be space to build a watery world with a pond and a waterfall spring, iris banks, lilies and reeds in the water, pebbles and sand on the bottom, and fish weaving through the underwater sunbeams.

Water can make a quiet ornament that gives the garden a meditative mood or a thrilling work of sound and movement. Before you choose, look through the first chapter, "Designing a Water Garden." It reveals the secrets of creating a stunning water garden, with or without plants and technology. The second chapter, "Building a Water Garden," describes the nitty-gritty of controlling mosquitoes, buying a pump, choosing a long lasting liner, keeping the water clear.

The "recipes," in the chapters that follow, contain all the information you need: lists of tools, materials, and plants, and the how-to steps for creating each water garden. The gardens are easy to build. The ones categorized as moderately difficult merely contain more steps than the others, or require more attention to detail or a certain level of confidence.

Because water is a precious resource, it doesn't feel right in any climate to place a tall fountain in an exposed place and watch the water vanish in the wind. But precisely because it's so precious, water makes an almost spiritual center to a garden. Displayed carefully and beautifully—perhaps just glittering and sparkling in an old bucket—water draws forth a sense of reverence for life, a sense of the garden being in right relationship with paradise.

DESIGNING A WATER GARDEN

Water is a decorative element in a garden. In design terms its role is to delight, to make a compelling stopping point, which it does easily. An ordinary puddle, replicable in a bucket of water, is extremely decorative: it glitters in the sunshine, ripples in a breeze, flickers with reflections of white petals in a spring green leafy smear, and pulls a piece of sky down next to the doorstep or the apple tree.

A small tank or a pond has room for a brown water lily bud nosing out of a cloud and unwinding into a spiky lemon cream cup, with a few goldfish to slide along under the lily pads, their orange tails disappearing into black-green water weeds stirring over dark pools. A fountain or waterfall adds sound; it will pull people out into the garden to catch sprays of crystal droplets flying against the sun.

STILL WATER AND REFLECTIONS
Still water, in a pond or a 6-inch-square piece of concrete footing, draws onto it light from the sky, reflections of treetops, the loops of the spider's web in the overhanging rose, the gold stamens among the petals. It dramatizes everything it reflects. Scenes and events that usually go unnoticed are captured in the water, wrapped in sunlight in a deep upside-down picture.

The picture can be bold and architectural. At Stourhead, in England, a copy of the Pantheon was built to reflect in one end of the lake, a Temple of Flora in the other. The Taj Mahal would be only half as romantic if its minarets and domes weren't reflected all through the very long canal in the entrance garden. Bridges double beautifully in the water below. A camelback Chinese bridge, seen from across the water, makes a moon, a symbol of perfection. Landscape architect Thomas Church rerouted a client's driveway around a lake to set up a picture of the house reflected in the water. It hangs there—a warmly lit mass of stone with an entrance portico, second-floor veranda, mansard windows, chimney pots—spread majestically across an infinitely deep sky. On a domestic modern scale, the picture spread across the water might be of a white canvas umbrella and a white iron bench against dark cypresses; or blue glazed urns, a long slatted bench with airy white flowers tangled through the seat, and the vivid blue window frames of the house.

Reflections of nature change with the light and the seasons. Reeds cast needle-thin lines way out across the water early and late in the day. After a storm, the bowed and broken tips strung with raindrops make black hooks and elbows among the horizontal ripples. A birch tree in spring-green leaf makes a fuzzy patch of reflection like a lime watercolor wash. In fall, as the leaves float down, the movement is mirrored in the water. During the winter, the white trunk and branches throw dramatic splayed stripes across the water between swaying skins of paper-thin yellow leaves and old catkin seeds.

If water is open to the sky, not shaded by trees or buildings, it will catch the light as it changes through the day. A bowl of water out in a sunny flower bed raised above the plants and open to the horizon will flush from rim to rim with gold and pink light at dusk, fading to silver and pewter and black as the evening star rises and back through those colors in the hour before daybreak. On cloudy days the light shifts tantalizingly, sunshine sweeping across the water, lighting it up in blinding sparkles then disappearing, a dazzling moment followed by more placid gray. When rain falls in slanting gray sheets, the water becomes choppy and pocked. If there's any hope of the rain stopping, you'll see the lightness in the sky run in a glistening sweep across the water.

Situating water so that it's open to the sky ensures the largest play of light across its surface, but dark water catches reflections too and produces a rare sense of mystery and tension as thrilling as moonlight. A bucket with a large rim set within the shadow of a tree will mirror giddy black branches backlit against the sky and big inky blotches of the underside of dense foliage pierced with silver spangles. On a gray day, dark water can be beautifully melancholy. Imagine a path leading through shady trees alongside a black pool of water, the air suddenly cooler and heavy with smells of damp soil and rot, then the path opening out onto a clean green lawn bordered with fragrant light-colored roses and phloxes and Queen Anne's lace. All great gardens have those modulations of mood and moments of tension. In a hot and bright climate, where a sheet of still water can dazzle relentlessly without much interest, shadowy places, under an arbor or tree, provide the best settings for quiet water.

Reflections vary according to the position of the light source in relation to the object and the eye. Buckets and bowls can be repositioned as the seasons change, but if you're planning a permanent reflection pool, it's worth experimenting with brimming buckets, or mirrors laid flat on the ground. Place them at different points around the garden and then check the reflections from various places, such as the main windows of the house, the entrance to the garden, stopping places along the path, and directly at the water's edge, from seat level as well as standing. The house might reflect beautifully from the bottom of the garden looking back, or the neighbor's satellite dish might ruin all the places along the fence. The reflections will change at different times of day and in different seasons, soft and clear with the light behind you, lost in the glare with the sun in front of you. If the reflections are less than perfect, think about creating your own. Position a tall urn at the edge of the pond to make its reflection on the water, or plant bamboo or a ranging, arching shrub like Chinese lantern. If the satellite dish shimmers smack in the middle of the water, put a water lily there to cover the reflection with its flat pads.

MOVING WATER 回回
Moving water animates a garden, brings it to life in a spectacle of flashing light and splashing sound. As it tumbles off the top of a fountain or slides over a rock into a pond, droplets and bubbles drip off the tips of grasses, wet the surrounding stones, or roll into the lily pads. Before it comes to rest, it sends waves running across the catchment area, breaking over pebbles and rocking up against the banks.

The commotion is a gentle one from a small pipe or a bubbler beneath pebbles in a bowl. It's soothing then, like trees soughing overhead on a windy day. In contrast, water spilling from basin to basin or soaring in a strong jet or gushing from a faucet makes a jubilant cacophony of slaps and splashes.

In hot climates, a riot of splashing water freshens the air. In a breezy place, if it's hot enough, people will welcome the spray and risk wetting their sleeves to cool off. In a damp sunless climate, it's generally agreed that fountains are chill and depressing, because the water falls without light sparkling through it and rocks about in the basin in stormy grayness. However, a small fountain, perhaps a pipe tipping water into a trough, seems fitting and lovely even in a cool climate. It's not a place to stop at for long, but the tinkle of water is merry, and as you pass by in thick clothes and boots you're reminded of a wild landscape: rainwater seeping out of banks, dripping down through foliage, watering the roots of violets, and chuckling its way downhill into ditch and drain. Such a feature builds harmony in the garden, links it with the gentle life-sustaining energy in the outside landscape.

Neither lilies nor fish like falling water, so choose a small fountain or a bubbler in a container or pond where you have them. Place it at the opposite side of the pond from the lilies; be sure there's a quiet place for the fish.

Start off with the water pressure low. Gushing water is irritating to many people's ears. It's a matter of personal taste, but, in a garden setting, gently flowing water, just a trickle like a meadow stream skipping over a stone, is more enjoyable than a roar like a waterfall during the spring snow melt. Rollicking water has a wild sound that evokes awe and fear, unnerving emotions close to the house. Set at a moderate trickle, water will not ride off the edge of the falls in one loud chute but instead slide off in several rivulets, each with its own pretty sound. Place a flat stone beneath one of the rivulets to further vary the sound.

I'm not fond of fountains where the water spurts out of the ground and disappears back through pebbles, or slides down a rock of slate into the patio floor. There's splash and glitter and coolness and patterns of wetness on the rock, but no pool of quiet water below. What is lost is the comforting sense of the water coming to rest, returning to the sea.

Choose a water sculpture carefully. The style and materials and scale must be right for your garden; the plantings around it will need to be sympathetic to its shape and color. Listen to the sound the water makes. Some water sculptures remain beautiful focal points when the water needs to be turned off on windy days or in cold-winter areas. Those with bowls, if they are frost-proof, can be left full to reflect the sky.

Ready-made "tabletop" fountains are extremely difficult to settle in. There's no natural place for a two-foot cascade in any garden. Better to improvise with a tin or bucket or concrete bowl and a piece of copper pipe or culvert, all common, hence natural-looking, objects in our environment. Bamboo, though beautiful with water (the sound echoes inside the pipe), is not really a common material here; plant a small grove or make a bamboo fence to make a Japanese *tsukubai* with a bamboo spout look at home.

WATER AS A FOCAL POINT

At the Little and Lewis water sculpture garden on Bainbridge Island, Washington, a tall urn sits surrounded by lawn, its fine shape accentuated by the space around it and the purple-stemmed, yellow-daisy-headed *Desdemona ligularia* that anchors it to its place in the grass. From the main approach, the urn is seen through an arch, which concentrates the view of it, adding drama. There's also interest close-to: plump crosses of pea green duckweed swim on the water surface, and orange light swells from inside the urn, sunbeams bouncing off the orange interior. And there's more interest around the urn: in late August, a black angelica heavy with seeding umbels and a final pancake-sized streaked blue and lavender clematis flower on the arch among fluffy beards of clematis seed and rosehips.

Focal points draw the eye. Set up properly, they do two things: lead people out into the garden and all the way through it, from one focus to the next; and, perhaps more importantly, make each area a distinctly satisfying place to stay for a while.

In his interior design book *The Essential House Book,* Terence Conran explains that a room without a focal point "is a strangely disconcerting one. There may be warmth, light, and a comfortable place to sit, but without a feature to which all eyes instinctively turn in moments of repose, it will never be a room in which people really feel at ease." The same is true of the garden. Indoors, a log fire is an unfailingly successful focal point; outdoors, people are drawn toward water by the same kind of primitive excitement and promise of comfort.

Walking round the urn at the Little and Lewis garden, a new focal point comes into view—an 8-foot-long rusty alligator lying on the grass in front of two black Adirondack chairs. There's no resting here for too long before the next focal point pulls one into the very back of the garden, onto a lawn in the shade of huge fir trees, where a waist-high water sculpture holds a reflection surface the size of a dining table up to the sky. Its interior is dark and twists down into a black tunnel that seems not to end. The mind either floats on the silver surface spread with reflections of black fir branches and clouds, or it drifts downward into the black depths. Four of us whiled away an hour leaning over this sculpture in the darkest part of the garden.

Walking back toward the main garden, into the light, past the urn, another water container comes into view through the arch. This one is a mass-produced pretty terra-cotta pot, raised on a concrete paver and settled back into the flowers in a large flower bed. Plants lean against and over the pot sides, softening the pot outline. A miniature water lily breaks and softens the shape of the water surface. Water is used discreetly here; even the pattern on the pot bows to the flower theme. But the sparkle on the water and the tall firm shape of the pot make a place among the vibrant flowers for the eye to rest. In a flower garden, a more visually dominant water feature, a fountain for example, might create a "too rich overtone," warned British designer Russell Page, "as though a wedding cake were waltzing."

A quiet eye of water in a raised pot or birdbath fits easily into a colorful garden. The grandest water features—tall classical fountains, modern water sculptures, waterfalls, ponds with rushes, lilies, and fish—have a far stronger presence of their own and may require a creative garden makeover. A classical carved fountain needs a formal space and formal materials around it, such as a circular or rectangular terrace made of aged brick or stone, and if the house is within view, it too needs something of a classical look or the fountain will be better hidden from it. Modern water sculptures need sympathetic surroundings that pick up on the color and shape and mood of the sculpture. Waterfalls need a hillside space or at least a berm, wild plantings, a damp atmosphere perhaps created by overhanging trees. Natural ponds need natural looking surroundings, such as rocks, grasses, and banks, and not a glimpse anywhere of an urban view.

Whether the focal point is a pot or a waterfall tumbling into a large pond, the design rule is simple: one focal point per view. If the entire garden is open and visible from the back deck, there's one opportunity for a focal point. To settle a new fountain into the space, an existing large rock garden planted with showy alpines will have to go. Alternatively, a second space can be created for the fountain, a side room or alcove taken out of view by a hedge or tall plants or a wall or a trellis.

The more areas in the garden, the more opportunities for focal points, and the easier it is to find places for old ornaments that don't fit the style of the new water feature. Each space may have its own style and mood. Multiple spaces, differently ornamented, are what make a garden feel interesting and spacious. And along the paths or set back into the hedges or at the entrances to new spaces there are opportunities for more water features, small surprises.

MINOR WATER SURPRISES 回回 The focal points in a garden are necessarily few, but there are many opportunities for small water details in most gardens: one or two sunken pockets of water in a rock garden double the depth of the cliff faces and reflect the flowers growing over the edge; a child's handmade clay rope pot collects rose petals among rose reflections at the foot of an arch; a bowl sunk under a holly bush by the path contains a sheen of ice melting in the morning sunshine among reflections of glistening red berries.

A garden looks impressively cared for if it has enchanting details in simple places. At the back door, up against a steep bank, a shady place most times of the day, a square concrete footing holds a few inches of water next to the porch post and a reflection of an iris just come into indigo bud. A companion plant will lend its reflections once the iris has finished flowering. Out in the vegetable garden, it's fun to dip a can into an old bucket or a new aluminum livestock trough to water the parsley. A garden faucet offers a grand opportunity to make a water garden—underneath it place a raised, brimming concrete trough or an old fifties sink nestled into a log.

George Little has an urn in the shadow of a banana tree, to pull you close under the leaves. The upside-down reflection of a pot of drooping love-lies-bleeding and the purple ribbed undersides of the tree is well worth stopping for on the way to the house from the Adirondack chairs on the lawn, not to mention the cozy feeling of shelter standing under the giant leaves. George particularly likes that spot; as a child he sheltered under his parents' banana trees in Texas during storms.

Moving water can also be downscaled to a minor surprise on the way to the main points of the garden. A mask spitting a splash of drops into a bowl within earshot of the deck needs no very special place of its own; you come upon it on the way out into the garden, set back into a wall of foliage, a moment's stopping place as you walk by. A bank makes an excellent place for a rough pipe dripping water onto ferns. It will look for all the world like rain-water percolating naturally out through the soil.

Designer Sharon Osmond finds potential water garden objects in dump trucks and scrap yards; she's looking for any container that's watertight, any sort of pedestal—any kind of ornament is fair game. At the turn of a path in her own garden, a mannequin hand rises out of a water bowl with pennywort in it; another hand is planted in the garden alongside. A dish sitting on a stool started out with a pattern of water lettuce, and then the ducks got in it—faded egg-yolk yellow plastic ones wobbling among live, pastel green, shell-shaped leaves. Pebbles are useful accessories for small water features, as are mossy stones, floating glass balls, and perhaps even gummy rubber toy alligators.

Look for containers with a fine silhouette or a broad rim. Jars, urns, and pots with gorgeous flowing sides are best seen in outline—against a plain backdrop, in the middle of mowed grass, not hidden among shrubs or flowers where their lines disappear. Raise them on concrete pavers or bricks if necessary to catch the outline; if they are placed low, only the neck will show. A pot with a generous rim will hold a large water surface and thus a large circle of light and reflections. Raise it enough so that it's open to the sky. More ordinary containers can be placed in pairs, their bases disguised with plants and their surfaces ornamented with aquatic plants or floating balls. A dark interior creates the best reflections; a light interior reveals the contours of the pot and any debris that has collected in the bottom. Don't limit your search to pots. Shallow black plastic cement-mixing trays are ideal for little ponds sunk into the ground, the edges disguised with grasses or pebbles or bricks. Any kind of metal tank will also do nicely.

DESIGNING WITH WATER PLANTS 回回 Water does not need to be dressed up much with plants. A clear pond creates a flat sheet of silver light and clouds, greatly expanding the sense of light and space in the garden. Once it's planted, the pond shrinks and keeps shrinking as the plants grow, until light no longer sparkles off the water and leaves have grown over where the cloud reflections once were. A heavily planted ditch loses its contours; there should be a clear view of the dark muddy bottom among the rushes, puddles lit up with spangles, places to watch water striders scoot between the stems.

Placing plants in water bowls can obscure their lovely shapes. Duckweed or water fern won't spoil the outline of an expensive old water jar, but taller plants may. A bowl with a generous width and a hand-turned rosy lip will lose half its beauty if plants cover the edges. An eighteenth-century font made of mossy Cornish granite filled with milky green water is probably most beautiful if left unplanted. In the same way, classical fountains with carvings and elegant ponds with stone or brick coping and cupids are rarely elaborated with water plants, especially not flowering ones; the play of light and shadow and sound, and the contrast between age-old stone and fleeting water, are more evocative than plants.

Restraint, though, is especially hard to master, because water plants are easy and exciting to grow. The little floaters grow as crazily as cress in a jar, forming larger and larger quilts on the water surface. Duckweed is a ¼-inch lime green cross. The four leaves of water clover are held together in a soft 1-inch square by a center the size of a pin. The abstract patterning of these plants works especially well in modern gardens where there's no pretense of the garden mimicking a natural landscape. Perhaps choose industrial materials for containers, a shiny ribbed aluminum tank, for example, at the entrance to a warehouse loft. Keep the water brimming to the top of the container; there's not only more water surface that way but also a sense of abundance and extravagance. Remove some of the plants almost monthly.

Water lily leaves, or pads, make a lovely pattern on the water if you allow them sufficient space. Once they bunch from overcrowding, gone is the lazy drifting pattern with water sparkling between the leaves. Like the little flat floaters, lily pads bob with the breeze and cast shadows in the water below. But being so large and canvas flat, they collect dewdrops and splashes in the centers, and their tips sometimes prick the bulging water surface so that the water douses the whole pad. The least showy flowers, the white or cream hardy species, blend more naturally with most garden landscapes than the blues and reds and purples. Use the vivid colors in a tropical garden, or treat them stylistically, as eye-stoppers in rectangular ponds or to pick up a color theme in the garden or the architecture.

In the most natural areas of the garden, far from the house, say, where the prim borders give way to woodland, the outline of the pond may be too strong to look right if you leave the water unplanted. Reeds, sedges, and water irises in pots in the water will blur the water's edge, and, if the bank is planted with soil-loving irises and grasses, the place where the water begins and ends will be beautifully mysterious. A few delicate sedges breaking the water surface produce fine, romantic lines in reflection. They catch any slight motion in the air or water. Raindrops slide down them; they crack in frost and tip back into the water. A gazebo or any piece of rustic architecture reflected in reedy water makes an extremely romantic picture. Build large ponds for tall reeds; choose grasses and dwarf reeds and sedges for smaller ponds.

Tall water plants with broad leaves, such as taro, arrowhead, and lotus, create loops of permanent shadow on the open water, like the dark pond edge under an overgrown bank. Reflections of the veined undersides of the leaves can be made out in the shadows. Light sometimes strikes off the water onto the undersides of the leaves, where it flickers in time with the water ripples. In a rainstorm the leaves act as umbrellas; water rolls and spills off the edges in a waterfall into the pond.

Pondweeds growing submerged in the water draw the eye off the water surface into its depths. They wave about like feelers and claws in a tide pool. It's mysterious what sets them in motion. Light catches their dark strands floating over a pond bed of pale sand and pebbles.

Think for a moment before planting pond chokers. Water hyacinth, pennywort, parrot's feather, and water lettuce quickly form thick blankets over the water, blocking reflections and the view down into the water. A pot can be emptied out (never into a natural waterway because these plants will become a nuisance there also), but a pond is harder to clear; oftentimes just a few missed pieces will grow into a new choking blanket. Until you're familiar with their habits in your climate, or until you know your love for them is long-lasting, plant them in containers. Water hyacinth is fragrant and has a bulbous stem base that tilts it like a buoy on the water; blue-green parrot's feather is ticklishly soft and delicate, half floating, half submerged; water lettuce is a pale pea green cluster of soft shell-shaped leaves.

If you're going to let plants get out of hand, let them be water lilies in a pond at the bottom of the garden. How gothic they look when you come across them lost among long grass and unpruned shrubs in an old estate garden, the pads bunched and tilted in green water, emerald algae swaying around them, the gardener long since gone away and the pond grown over with glorious flowers as if in a dream!

The most notable water gardens are usually the simplest. If you become a water plant collector, become also a collector of water containers. Experiment with one or two plants per pot, and place the pots either individually through the garden as minor surprises or in a group as a focal point. If you plan to plant a pond, be sure to make it extra large; leaves steal over the surface fast. Even in the realm of pots, think big. That way there's room for the water cannas to grow luxuriantly, with plenty of uncovered water surface to double their purple stems and orange flowers among the clouds.

ACCESS TO THE WATER

As soon as the eye spots water or the ear hears it, the mind sets the feet in motion. Children will rush right to the water, as long as there's no planting or other obstacle in their way, and have their arms crooked over the bowl and trailing through the water as deep as they can reach; they'll taste it unless they're stopped and splash each other's faces and stamp in the spill on the ground. Access all around a fountain and right to its edge provides an opportunity to feel the spray and skip over the place where it's blowing onto the paving. A can or bowl on the edge is an invitation to dip it into the commotion and cool off up to the wrists.

Place urns, troughs, and buckets within reach—at the path edge or alongside a seat. If the water surface is high off the ground, either in a tall container or in a pot raised on a pedestal, it's easier to touch.

A pond needs a bench or a tree stump or a crate or other seating somewhere on its boundary. The most alluring place is a wide rim seat low and close to the water edge, within arm's reach of the water so that it can be stirred or swished about with a stick, or contemplated for the time it takes for a fish to reappear from the pondweeds or for the sunlight to emerge from behind a wisp of mist and light up the sand on the bottom.

A bridge across the pond—a plank or stepping-stones look most natural—offers a view from above the water and from the far bank. Bridges don't make sense and lose much of their appeal if there's another obvious way around to the far bank, so close off the view of any such path with shrubs or reeds.

A promontory offers something of the same thrill of being out in the water. The most tantalizing water I've ever seen was in a photograph in the *New York Times Magazine* (February 4, 1996) of Charles Jencks's paisley-shaped lake with a thin narrowing strip of plain grass swirling far out into it. The water looks as if it brims right up to the grass strip. Walking out to the tip must feel like almost walking on water. In a small garden, a stepping-stone in the middle of the pond suggests a similar kind of bold journey. If you have a kidney-shaped pond, place a boulder on the tip of the promontory so that there's a place to sit out there almost surrounded by water. The boulder will make the kidney shape more natural looking, as if the water had to swing out around the rock.

Limiting access to the water creates mystery. A far bank with a waterfall on it, a bush of fragrant white angel's trumpets, and no obvious access sets the imagination looking for landing places. A hidden point of access generates surprise: a path might follow one edge of a wide ditch, veer away from it, and then jag back to the edge just where a bush had hidden two narrow planks across the water. Or perhaps the ditch is planted densely on both sides and feels maddeningly inaccessible until the path swings suddenly over it on a bridge.

Alone at landscape architect Jack Chandler's place, I searched all across one side of the property for access to the tantalizingly secret-looking pond over the garden wall below the house windows. The sun was going down, the fall color on the hillside was drawn across the water, and a painted boat had caught my eye on a small beach. Finding not even a suggestion of a path, I hurried back down the driveway, glanced around furtively, then scrambled over the wall and pushed through the grasses and reeds to the water's edge. I had walked rather rudely into a tableau meant to be seen only from afar: the pond was in fact small, the scale camouflaged by the reeds and the hillside reflections and the boat, which turned out to be one of Jack's sculptures, perhaps half the size of a skiff. There was also a practical reason for cutting off the pond from the house: rattlesnakes in the grasses.

PLANTS ON THE WATER'S EDGE 回回 Out in the country near where I live, in the garden of a residence built of industrial metal to mimic the neighboring dairy barns, a raised concrete pond sits on a decomposed granite courtyard, collecting watercolor reflections of the green and gold hillside and the bright blue California sky. It's a centuries-old design from Persia and Europe: the water placed centrally and uncluttered by plantings, so that it's open to the play of light from dawn to dusk and visible and accessible from the garden on all sides.

Bushy trees on the water's edge shut off the view of the water, creating a more private place. A ring of them makes a dramatic vault over a dark mysterious pool; a fountain there would catch any glints of sunlight streaking through the trees. Lines of clipped hornbeams bordering water cast reflections of their straight trunks across the surface and leave the view of the water open below the foliage. Before planting trees alongside water, investigate how much litter they'll drop. The water will foul unless you clean out the leaves frequently or place a net over the surface.

Low neat plants around a formal pond emphasize its lines. Paving in the same material as the pond edge also plays up the formality. A little looseness might be introduced by planting creeping thyme between the pavers and letting blowsy vines arch and sweep over a nearby wall.

Simple greenery and paving complement water. Foliage, stone, and water make the classic compositions seen in Paris parks and many of the old estate gardens in Europe. A circular pond with jet fountains sits in a gravel terrace bounded by lawn, yew hedges, and woodland. A gargoyle spits water from an ivy clad wall into a basin decorated only with moss. Foliage plantings and open space around the water feature heighten the drama of the water, make it the point to which the eye instinctively turns.

Plants can help tie an informal pond to the landscape. Instead of ringing the water with an unnatural looking necklace of grasses or same-size boulders (one looks immediately for the liner the gardener is trying to disguise), bring drifts of tall plants from the garden down to the water's edge on one side, and on the other take slab stones or lawn right to the edge. On the viewing side, water stretches away uninterrupted from one's feet, and the plants on the far bank appear in reflection on the water.

Plants also help settle other water elements into the garden. The base of a freestanding fountain might be disguised with a ring of ferns and moss; they collect drops spilling from the lowest bowl, and lend an appropriate sense of moisture to the site. If an urn seems a little stark and lonely set in the middle of the lawn, anchor it with a plant at its base. To play up a watery atmosphere, choose large-leaved moisture-loving plants, such as ornamental rhubarb, umbrella plant, and rodgersia; they contrast dramatically with slim reeds in the water.

FISH 回回 Fish add movement and color to a water garden and draw attention to the quiet world under the surface. They flash gold under green-black weeds, glide over sandy beaches lit by bent sunbeams wobbling through the waves, race in shoals past underwater rocks.

Two or three goldfish or shubunkins will be happy in a deep pot; they'll feed on plants and mosquito and midge larvae. If you want to see shoals of fish swimming out of the gloom into the shallows, design a pond specially for them, with some deep areas for overwintering and protection from raccoons.

It's possible to keep one or two koi in the large ponds described in this book, but koi are a specialized business, best left to people prepared to make a serious commitment. They grow quickly, and to stay healthy they need very fresh clean water, passed through large filtering units, and daily care.

NATURAL DESIGNS 回回 In nature, water collects at the bottom of a slope, in an irregularly shaped pool that follows the contours of the land. Waterfalls occur on wet, steep, rocky land, and at the base is a pool, before the water flows on, over another fall or into a stream. Geysers appear on low land, the pressure formed from the weight of water above. Ditches follow the course of rushing water seeking the easiest way downhill, skirting boulders and trees and banks.

I once visited a garden where a kidney-shaped "natural" pond sat precariously on the edge of a view 30 miles down over the hillside to the sea. It looked as if it must surely spill and drain in a minute. On the other side of the house, set back into the hilltop, where water might naturally have collected, it would have been more credible. As you plan a water feature, think of the most likely source of water on your site and where water might naturally drain. A bank or ditch is a godsend for a water gardener. On a flat site, a waterfall is impossible to accommodate naturally, but a fountain is plausible.

Water in an unnatural place jars one's visual sensibilities, but unless you're out in the countryside and your garden has water already flowing through it, there's little chance of creating an entirely natural-looking water feature. Better to abandon the notion and think of the garden the way landscape designers do: as a created and intentional space, halfway between the house and nature. Thomas Church introduces his famous book *Gardens Are for People* with this idea. The Egyptians, Romans, Greeks, and Renaissance Italians all "borrowed line and materials from the house; and they borrowed foliage, shade, fruit, flowers, and the play of water from nature. It was a subtle compromise. . . . The garden was a transitional stage saving them from the embarrassment of stepping from their house to nature in the raw."

Gardening becomes easier with this philosophy. A rectangular, brick-edged pond sits so well at the edge of the straight-sided patio, the lines continued out from the house, no awkward spaces caused by a kidney shape swinging in and out alongside a straight line. You don't need to do as much fabrication, screening out the garden's boundary lines and the buildings in view, or moving earth to make the land match the style of the water. The same applies to flowing water: a faucet and an oblong trough, unashamedly unnatural objects, sit next to the garden fence quite naturally.

There's opportunity for a loose natural effect even with a geometric shape. Several Oehme and van Sweden ponds have a clean brick or stone edge where they meet the patio and far edges lost in sedges that merge the water with the meadow of grasses beyond.

A clear rectangle of water set along the length of the garden elongates the space, makes the garden look longer. Set across the garden, it widens the space, drawing the eye to both edges. Squares and circles are static shapes; they draw attention from the surroundings, localizing the view, limiting the sense of space, but they're useful if you're trying to keep the focus in the garden and away from urban surroundings. An oval is a lovely shape for water: not as static as a circle, and offering an outline that changes—sometimes almost round, sometimes very elliptical—depending on the viewing point.

Designs that suit a moist gray climate may rankle in a dry garden. Pools of placid water open to the sky look lovely in damp rolling green grass swards; they catch the light on a gray day and split the mild landscape open with deep reflections of clouds. In sunny arid climates, such a pool would blind with dazzle and make most people shudder with distress over the evaporation. In the chapters that follow, there are designs for every kind of water feature— ponds, economical pots and urns and jars, springs, ditches—and also playful gardens that are actually entirely dry but tease the imagination into seeing water, such as dry creeks running over river rocks, a smooth shiny globe blazing with reflections, a blue flower bed that ripples with light like a canal.

BUILDING A WATER GARDEN

Water gardening can be very simple. You can drop frogbit into a tank of water and forget about it until its white three-petaled flowers open among the tiny pads in late summer. If debris has collected on the water and you don't like it as a water skin, you can tip the tank out and refloat the flowering frogbit on fresh water. It will come back next year on its own accord, its overwintering buds rising from the tank bottom and expanding on the warm light-streaked water in spring.

This chapter contains information that might draw you on to stocking the tank with waterweeds and a few fish to create a watery world that's inhabited and changing, like a pocket of wild water. Or perhaps it will give you the confidence to shop for a pump, to add to the tank the proven stress-reducing sounds of a fountain splashing. Equipment for a water garden is no harder to use than kitchen equipment; it's fun shopping for it, picking out the fittings for the pump, screwing in a T-piece, deciding to go for the elbow piece that's less than a dollar in case you want to turn the waterspout sideways so the spring bubbles up under a stone. Water gardening is easy, and chemicals aren't necessary, even to get the better of algae.

AQUATIC PLANT BASICS

All plants need two elements: light and water. Place your water garden where it will receive sun, the more the better, and the plants will have both essential elements in abundance. Catalogs give specifications about water depths over roots and sell special pots for aquatics, but you really can't go far wrong; aquatic plants don't drown. The most common problem is too-rapid growth resulting in colonization of the sparkling water surface.

As you plant in a bowl or pond, think of yourself as a steward of the water environment. Your main job is to keep the water unpolluted, so that the plants and fish will be safe and healthy. Watch that mortar doesn't get into the water, because it contains lime, which damages plants and kills fish. Old bricks sometimes have cement traces on them; use clean bricks to support submerged pots. Lime is also present in cinder blocks. To keep insecticides and fungicides out of the water, remove sick plants or fish to a separate water hospital, and treat them there.

Your second job is to stop excessive amounts of nutrients from building up in the water, because that's the cause of algae. Again, it's a matter of watchfulness, that's all. Use plain, heavy, unamended and unsprayed garden soil in your planting pots. Don't think of spoiling aquatic plants with the rich peaty mix that regular garden plants love; the particles will float out, muddy the water, and release a lot of nutrients for the algae. For the same reason, bury fertilizer pellets—always use pellets, never liquids or amendments—deep inside the pots.

For plant pots, the best are probably the solid black plastic ones. They are light to handle, and the color disappears against the bottom of the water garden. Tests have shown that there's no advantage to the fiddly exercise of lining baskets with burlap or cutting holes in the sides or bottoms of the pots. Aquatic plants thrive in waterlogged conditions, obviously. If your pots have small holes already, that's all right; large holes need to be covered, because soil will float out and muddy the water, and fish will nibble the plant roots—this is also the reason pea gravel is placed in the top of the pot. The roots of aquatic plants grow laterally rather than down, so use shallow, wide pots; aquatic plant suppliers sell them. Dish-washing pans will do; they're just the right shape, or regular plastic garden pots cut down to half their height. Waterlogged terracotta pots become heavy and slippery; redwood containers spoil the water.

Because aquatic plants often grow so aggressively that they become pests, plant all aquatics (except of course the surface floaters) in containers. If plants start to root outside the pots in the debris on the water floor, catch and stop them while you can. Give extras to friends or compost them; never set them free in a natural waterway, where they might become a vast nuisance. If you're making a basin or pond with a liner, avoid the few plants, such as cattails, that have invasive sharp piercing roots.

SURFACE FLOATERS, SUBMERGED OXYGENATORS

Floaters and submerged oxygenators are the most watery aquatics, to my mind. Patterned with floaters, the water heaves and ebbs visibly when a dragonfly leaves a reed. Oxygenators move with the motions that take place under the water; they draw the eye down into the depths.

Both kinds of plants are hardworking water garden components. The small hardy floaters—duckweed and water fern—spread quickly, shading the water in spring when other plants are still dormant and the light promotes algae blooms. They shouldn't, however, be allowed to cover more than 70 percent of the water surface if you have fish or want room for reflections, so be careful about letting them loose on a large pond; you'll never be able to net enough to keep them under control, though goldfish will nibble away at duckweed. Planting floaters is a matter of dropping them onto the water surface; their roots trail through the water.

Oxygenators don't actually produce much oxygen, but they absorb minerals and carbon dioxide, thus cleaning the water and outcompeting algae (all water plants have this cleaning effect, but none so strongly as the oxygenators). Planting in submerged pots one bunch for every 2 or 3 square feet of water surface is the best way to keep your water clear and fresh. Fish nibble on the stems, so plant the oxygenators a month before introducing the fish, to give the plants a chance to get established. Plant a mix of species, because some are temperamental, five bunches per pot, and place them completely underwater. Don't fertilize them.

BOG PLANTS AND MARGINALS

Bog plants love moist soil but not waterlogged conditions, so they will not grow *in* water. Some, such as ornamental rhubarb, rodgersia, many of the iris species, and bog primula, are common enough water-loving plants to suggest the presence of water. If you live in a moist climate or are willing to irrigate the garden around the water feature heavily, you can grow banks or swales of these and paint a grand water picture across the garden.

Marginals are water plants. They grow in water, their roots completely submerged and most of their foliage above the water surface. Marginals include tall thin green horsetails, catttails, thalias, and bulrushes, bright flowering water cannas and water irises, and little lilylike white or yellow snowflakes and floating hearts.

Plant marginals in large pots, very large pots if you want the very largest plants. The plant label will specify how many inches of water the plant needs over the top of the pot. You do not need a pond with shelves, or a pond at all, to grow marginals (they never look natural ringed around a shelf anyway). Place them in any kind of watertight container, and raise them to the right height on clean bricks. Water fur, the sediments from the water, will camouflage bricks and pots in no time.

WATER LILIES 🔲🔲
Water lilies are either hardy or tropical. Tropical water lilies are the less common type. They produce flowers above the pond, often in star shapes rather than cups, and often intensely fragrant. Some tropical water lilies bloom at night. The colors range into strange neon pastel blues and purples. They bloom in midsummer, when the water temperature exceeds 70 degrees at night. Frost will kill them, so in cold-winter climates treat them as annuals or store the tubers wrapped in dark plastic, kept moist, in a frost-free place. Hardy water lilies are rarely more than slightly fragrant, but they will come back year after year as long as the water doesn't freeze on the pond bottom.

Choose a small or medium water lily, according to the size of your water garden, a large-spreading variety only if you have a farm pond. Plan to cover about half the water surface with floating leaves. Nearly all lilies need at least six hours of direct sun to bloom heavily all summer long, but there are a few glorious lilies that will flower in shade. Most lilies will grow with as little as 6 inches of water over the tops of their pots or as much as 18 inches.

Lilies are demanding in two respects: the crowns (where the growing stems meet the tuber or rhizome) must sit slightly above the soil or gravel surface in the pots when you're planting them, and the roots like to feed heavily and regularly on specially formulated lily fertilizer pellets.

Plant lilies as soon as they're available in spring to get a lot of blooms in the first summer. Plant them in large containers, at least 12 inches in diameter.

WATER LOTUS 🔲🔲
Water lotus need enough summer heat to push the water temperature over 80 degrees, a planting pot 2 to 3 feet in diameter, and a couple of years to get established. With those matters settled, they are as easy to grow as water lilies, to which they are related. The blooms, and sometimes the leaves, rise well above the water surface. The flowers have a

musky fragrance, and, when they fall, the flower center turns slowly into an unforgettable brown seedpod that rattles with pea-sized seeds. Choose a dwarf variety, plant and care for it as you would a water lily, but feed it even more heavily.

ALGAE, KEEPING THE WATER CLEAR 回卍

Water can become polluted, and eventually sour-smelling, but algae aren't the cause of that. Algae are plants. Some algae are microscopic and cloud the water a milky pea soup green; stringy filamentous kinds drift through the water and settle under lily leaves or on underwater stems; sometimes, algae form into hand-sized patches of spongy froth.

Algae are natural, even pretty, if you can get away from the false notion that they mean the water is dirty. They grow prolifically—that's the main set-back—so they do need to be weeded out of water gardens occasionally, just as you'd weed scarlet pimpernel from a flower bed. The filamentous and spongy kinds can be pulled out by hand—wear gloves if you prefer, but algae are silky rather than messy to the touch, or net them with a small aquarium net.

Pea soup algae are harder to eliminate from the water. A water garden in a small bowl can be started over by emptying the water out, scrubbing the bowl with a stiff brush (no cleaners) and setting the plants back into fresh water. In larger water gardens it makes no sense at all to bail or pump out the water, because fresh water will bloom with algae again soon, and the water you will have thrown out may have been beautifully well balanced for the health of your fish and plants.

Algaecides offer a kind of solution for fountains with no plants or fish in the bowls. The true water quality, as measured by plants and fish in the water, is not an issue then (but check the label for the effect on birds), and algaecides will certainly kill pea soup algae and take the green hue out of the water if you use them regularly. Unfortunately, algae don't just vanish on contact with algae-cide; they decompose, making a mess in the water. In water environments with plants and fish, algaecides are not the answer to an algae problem; at best they are a very temporary solution—expect the algae back, undiminished.

My suggestion is to devise a simple battle plan against algae, and then pull out the occasional string or sponge algae that will doubtless appear anyway, and try to appreciate any pea soup algal bloom as a rare and interesting nat-ural feature of the water garden—it happens only at certain moments in the water cycle, and reflections on algae clouds are a beautiful soft green, reminiscent of natural ponds in woods.

Fight algae by introducing fish and plants into the water garden (fish eat algae and plant leaves absorb the nutrients that the algae need) and by preventing the conditions in which algae thrive—light all over the water and nutrients all through it. Shade the water surface by growing lilies or floaters; for the clearest water, cover as much as half of the water surface. To reduce nutrients, use only pellet fertilizers, and bury them in the plant pots, prevent garden water from spilling into the water garden, don't feed your fish (or feed them lightly and remove any food not eaten in five minutes), and clean up leaves and debris before they decompose. That kind of care will keep the water clear almost all year. In spring, when the water warms and the water plants are still dormant so the surface is flooded with light, expect a burst of algae. Be patient; as the other plants shade the water and the fish start feeding, the water will clear. Expect a similar algal bloom when you first fill the water garden; don't replace the water—the algae will recur.

Filters will draw algae and excess nutrients from the water, but won't remove every bit, especially if you are feeding fish. A biofilter is most effective.

Foul-smelling water is rare. Either it's been seriously polluted or it's been neglected so badly that a thick layer of organic matter is decomposing anaerobically on the bottom. Start over with entirely fresh water only as a last resort; leaving a quarter of the water, if it's not chemically polluted, will help the new water achieve a balance more quickly, like a starter dough.

GOLDFISH 回回 Goldfish are beautiful, useful—they eat mosquito larvae and algae—and quite hardy if you follow a few guidelines: Wait a few weeks after you've set up the water garden before introducing the fish, to give the chlorine in tap water a chance to clear; start with just two goldfish for a large container or six for a pond, so that there's plenty of oxygen in the water for them; buy the ordinary kind, not the more fragile fancy species; and feed the fish either not at all or only once a month, lightly, because their waste and uneaten fish food will fill the water with nutrients for algae. If you can take that approach, the fish will probably thrive without your making any special arrangements for them.

If you'd like lots of fish and you want to feed them, buy a filter, preferably a biofilter, to help keep the water clear. A waterfall or a fountain, or a fountain pipe set just below the water surface, will keep the oxygen level up in the water but isn't necessary. In cold-winter climates, you'll need a pond that's 30 inches deep for the fish to survive and a plan to keep part of the water surface free of ice so that toxic gases can escape; alternatively, overwinter the fish in an aquarium. Koi have even greater requirements; consult a professional before even starting to build the pond.

Buy your goldfish from someone who knows about fish. Choose fish 3 to 5 inches long that are lively and free of furry white patches (fungus) or damaged tails or fins. If there are inactive or obviously diseased fish in the tank, choose from a different tank. Buy fish that have been around for a while; the freshly imported fish may be diseased, and there's no way of telling.

The supplier will likely give you the fish in a plastic bag inflated with oxygen. Store it in a cool dark place on the way home. At the water garden, float the closed bag on the water for twenty minutes so the fish can adjust to the new water temperature before you slip them out. If it's a hot day, cover the bag with a cloth, to prevent it from heating up. Expect the fish to hide on the pond bottom for a few days while they acclimate.

WATER GARDEN CONTAINERS, SHELLS, LINERS

Water gardening containers are available everywhere. Check out aquarium stores as well as water garden nurseries, but also builders' supply yards, antique stores, urban recycling centers. Anything watertight will do for a reflection pond; a hubcap makes an interesting shallow silver bowl; a black cement-mixing tray is perfect for a small sunken pond that supplies a water pipe. Something with a patina of age will make the water garden look as if it's been there forever. A shiny glazed pot will always look squeaky clean. In cold-winter areas, ask whether a terra-cotta pot is frost-proof. If it's not, you'll need to empty it and store it during the winter (see page 41 for overwintering plants indoors).

Containers with holes can be plugged with corks and silicon caulking. Holes for waterspout pipes can easily be drilled into most things, even gargoyles. Avoid copper and lead containers or fittings if you plan to have fish. Avoid treated wood, redwood, and any container that has held dirty material—real wine barrels leach wine into the water and are difficult to keep watertight unless the staves are always well soaked along their entire length. Buy huge containers at least 20 inches deep for water lilies and other large aquatic plants, so the plants can spread without covering the entire water surface.

Preformed pond shells look reassuringly finished compared with a roll or pond liner, but shells take more work and care to install than liners and cost more. Choose a heavy-duty black shell with a guaranteed long life. (Flimsy shells are much more likely than the expensive rigid ones to buckle once they're holding water, and as the material becomes brittle with age, they will split.) Buy a large shell; although it seems huge on the Jeep roof rack, it dwarfs as it goes into the ground and becomes miniature once plants are placed on the banks or in the water.

A shell without shelves is far easier to install, because you can dig simple straight sides for it instead of excavating precise contours to exactly match the shell outline; the contours must be precise because the shelves must be well supported or the shell may buckle once the enormous weight of the water pushes against its surfaces. Check that the shell rim is level before you buy it. Think twice before buying a wiggly-edged shape; could water ever have collected naturally in such a shape in your garden? A simple rectangle is more visually appropriate in most gardens, and putting plants in and around the water will obscure the edges if you don't want a formal pond.

During the installation process, check and recheck that the shell is settling level, and backfill and compact damp sand around the shell sides as you fill the shell with water, so the sides won't bulge and sag unsupported from the water weight. As you edge it, keep heavy objects off the rim to prevent the pond from buckling; bricks are not heavy enough to damage the rim, but boulders should be either in the water or out of it and not touching the rim.

Liners, like preformed shells, need to be made of materials with a guaranteed long life, such as PVC, butyl, or EPDM. They come in different thicknesses; if you can, buy the thickest, because it will last the longest. Liners are easy to carry home and fairly easy to install to any shape you choose. Buy only black liner; it's the least visible once installed.

A pad of underlayment beneath the liner (on the pond bottom, and, if you like, also on the pond sides) helps protect the liner from puncture. A layer of old carpet pieces works just as well, and a thick layer of newspaper is better than nothing. It's best not to even consider putting a liner pond where brambles were or close to uncontained bamboo; their root tips are sharp and invasive. Some aquatic plants also have sharp roots and should not be placed in a liner pond.

As you excavate the hole for a liner, slope the pond sides slightly toward the pond bottom so they stay stable; loose soil needs a greater slope than heavy stable soils. Compact the sides and take care not to crumble them as you move in and out of the excavation. Shelves need to be particularly firm.

Once you have the liner draped in the pond and the edges secured by weights, start to fill the pond with water, which will push out some of the liner creases. Smooth the remaining creases into the corners. At the corners, treat the liner like a bed sheet; make one large pleat, and tuck it flat into the corner. A supplier will often demonstrate how to make the liner lie perfectly flat. If the pleats don't come easily, not to worry; try to smooth the liner next to the access to the pond, where people will be standing, and wait for the inevitable layer of water fur to cover up the details. Don't trim the liner until the pond has settled for a week.

Calculate the amount of liner you'll need by adding twice the pond depth, and 2 feet for overlap, to the pond width and length. For a pond 4 feet by 6 feet and 2 feet deep, you'll need a liner that is 10 feet wide (4 + 2 + 4) and 12 feet long (4 + 2 + 6).

Water looks good at a low point in the garden, because it might have collected there naturally. Be careful, though, about putting a pond shell or liner or tank in the way of a lot of water draining through the soil. Even when the pond is full of heavy water, pressure from water flowing through the ground against the pond can pop the pond up out of the ground. You might weight the pond with a layer of pebbles in the bottom, but in wet climates or wet soils, seek professional advice about rerouting the draining water around the pond.

WATER PUMPS 回回 You'll need a pump for any kind of fountain or spring. For small water gardens, all the ones described in this book, choose a submersible pump (not a surface, or exterior, pump). A submersible pump is silent and never needs priming. You can just drop it into the water (on top of a brick to keep silt out of the pump) and plug the cable into an electrical outlet. You can keep it running all the time or switch it on and off; it doesn't matter, as long as it's covered with water.

A T-piece on the pump outlet is so convenient it's almost a necessity. It contains a flow adjuster, so you can change the height of the fountain jet on windy days, or tinker with the sound of the water. It also provides a second outlet, to which you can attach a long piece of pipe if you ever need to pump some of the water out of the water garden, to clean it or make a repair. (The simplest fountain is nothing more than a T-piece with a plastic fountainhead pushed onto the top.)

Some pumps have a small pre-filter built in; this is no great advantage, because you can make a more effective filter by placing the pump inside a pot filled with gravel (see page 38).

Seek the supplier's guidance on two issues. Ask about the best manufacturer of the size of pump you need, and ask if you can return the pump if it turns out not to be sufficiently powerful for your water garden. You may decide after following a recipe carefully that you want the flow stronger or that the antique pipe you're using kinks the hose and reduces the flow. Adding a large filter or a different fountain jet, extending the hoses, or wanting the water to spill over a wide lip on a waterfall will also require a greater water flow and hence a larger pump.

The recipes in this book list the required pump size in gallons per hour (GPH) when the pump is full open or at maximum flow. If the recipe lists a 170-GPH pump, you may find just what you need in a pump called a P-170. However, some manufacturers' model numbers correspond not to maximum GPH, but to GPH at 1 or 2 feet above the water surface (the GPH drops rapidly the higher the water is lifted). You need not make any calculations about water lift if you're following a recipe; simply match the recipe recommendation with the maximum or full-open GPH on the pump performance chart.

If you like to work things out for yourself, you can make a good estimate of the pump performance you'll need by measuring the vertical distance from the pond to the spill at the waterfall (the lift, or head) and calculating the required GPH by placing a hose on the waterfall lip and measuring the flow in gallon buckets with a stopwatch. Or, for a small bubbler in a bowl, calculate the distance from the surface of the catchment tank that holds the pump to the top of the bubbler pipe, insert a hose into the bowl until the water is washing over the rim prettily on all sides, and measure that hose flow with a gallon bucket and stopwatch.

Once you have a pump in place in an actual water garden, water flow is affected by many factors. The pump recommendations in the recipes will give you some extra flow to play with, even when the tubings are a little clogged or kinked and the pump screen a little blocked. A pump that will perform properly only under ideal conditions requires constant maintenance and will probably not last, so buy big.

To make the most efficient use of your pump, buy good-quality accessories. Thick-walled hoses, especially the spirally reinforced ones, are superior to flimsy hoses, because they will turn corners without kinking and are less likely to get squeezed closed by a heavy pebble. Buy opaque hoses rather than clear plastic ones; where they are exposed to light, clear hoses may become clogged with algae. Hoses are sold by the diameter of the inside. If your pump outlet is ½ inch, you'll need a ½-inch-diameter hose, or, for the greatest efficiency, a ⅝-inch hose. Going up a size or two ensures less friction against the water flow. Secure hoses to the pump with barbed fittings, or wire or clamps if you prefer.

If you're adapting a recipe significantly—adding a large filter or a complex fountainhead, or substituting a waterfall for a bubbler—ask a supplier for advice on pump size. He or she may ask you about the volume of water in your feature. Calculate that by multiplying the length of the container by the width by the depth (all in inches), and then *dividing* the number by 231, to turn cubic inches into gallons; for a large pond, do the calculation in feet, and *multiply* by 7.5.

Before you buy a pump, make sure the cable is long enough to reach from the bottom of the pond to the electrical outlet. If you need a longer cable, ask the supplier for a pump with a long one fitted. Keep a record of where the cable is buried; anyone excavating the garden in the future will need the information. Disconnect the pump from the outlet before cleaning it or doing any kind of repair.

As the last step in installing the pump, read about the maintenance required. The screen at the water intake will need to be kept clear. If the water flow starts to dwindle, the flow is blocked and needs to be fixed immediately. However carefully you treat a pump, if it has a motor it rarely lasts more than a year or two; the ones with magnetic drives have the longest guarantees. A pump will die an almost instant death from corrosion if it comes into contact with bleach. If you want to clean your water garden, do it with a stiff brush, no cleaners.

STRAINERS, SCREENS, AND FILTERS 回回 Most submersible pumps have a screen on the water intake, which prevents large debris such as leaves from entering the pump. If you keep the intake clear and raise the pump off the bottom of the pond on a brick so that it doesn't draw in silt, that's a sufficient filtering system for many water gardens.

A pre-filter on the pump helps prevent the intake screen from blocking, so you don't need to check it so often. If there's no pre-filter on your pump, it's very easy to make one. Simply place the pump in a plastic basket or pot filled with rinsed pea gravel or 1-inch pebbles. The debris will collect in the gravel or pebbles, without affecting the flow of water into the pump. Once or twice a season, or more often if you see the fountain dwindling, disconnect the pump at the electrical outlet, remove the basket, and hose down the gravel. Leave a little debris and slime if you can, because it contains bacteria that eat pea soup algae in the water as they move through; if you hose all the debris off, it will take longer for the bacteria to reestablish. Because of this "biological" filtration effect, which helps clear the water, it's wise not to clean a pre-filter too often (but it mustn't be left so dirty that it blocks water flowing to the pump).

Biofilters are algae-eating factories. They contain materials with an enormous amount of surface area, not only to strain out particles mechanically but also for the microscopic algae to settle on and be eaten by the bacteria that are cultured in the biofilter. If you have a lot of fish or a perennial problem with green water, a biofilter will keep the water close to crystal clear, year round. Discuss the maintenance requirements with the supplier, consider the size of the unit and where you might conceal it, and make sure the pump is large enough to be reliable.

ELECTRICITY 回回 All pumps need electricity. Small submersible ones—for the recipes in this book—come with a waterproof cable and a three-prong plug that you simply plug into an electrical outlet. In the United States, most small submersible pumps run on the same voltage (115 volts) as regular house appliances; the very smallest are 24 volt and come with a transformer that plugs into the outlet.

If you have an outdoor weatherproof electrical box, you can plug the pump cable into that. The cable between the pump and the outlet probably need not be buried in a deep trench (check local code with an electrician or a local pump supplier), but it's sensible to bury it deeply if anyone is likely to dig the ground or use a rotary cultivator nearby. For safety's sake, always place the cable in a PVC conduit (wide enough for the plug to slip through it so you don't need to remove the plug first).

If there's no electrical box in your garden, consider having an electrician put one in, and at the same time install a switch so that you can turn the fountain or spring on and off from inside the house. The outdoor circuit probably needs a ground fault circuit interrupter (GFI, or GFCI) to meet local code. The electrician will know about that. For safety's sake, have the GFI installed, because it will shut off the current if it's interrupted—by a pet gnawing the cable or a child piercing it accidentally with a pocket knife. Make sure the box really will protect the wiring from weather—it needs to have a cover that you can close completely when the plug is plugged in. Place the box close to the water feature and hide it with plants, or place it against a wall or fence and bury the cable to the water garden.

Could you manage without an outdoor electrical box, by taking the pump cable through a hole under a window and plugging it into a house socket? It's against code or it should be, because it's potentially dangerous.

RACCOONS AND HERONS

Raccoons come to water gardens to eat—not only fish but water lily flowers, leaves, and tubers—and sometimes just to play, to knock bowls over and strew plants and hoses about on the ground. A black plastic net over the surface will stop them from fishing, and an electric fence around the water garden will protect everything. Other than those unsightly solutions, it's a matter of designing a water garden with raccoon obstacles built in. Raccoons won't swim for their supper, so fish and plants are safe if they are out of reach from the water's edge and the bank is steep; raccoons will wade in from a beach or a flat stone. Plants in the water and a deep spot away from the edge give fish places to hide.

Herons have a long reach with their bills, but they usually (exceptions abound) won't enter the water unless they can wade in from a beach. If you have problems with herons, consider setting up a 6 inch high fence of black thread or fishing line tied to twig poles pushed in among plants on the bank. The herons will try to approach the water and perhaps be frightened off by the invisible barrier. The notion that a heron sculpture will convince the real birds (who prefer feeding in solitude) to stay in flight is probably nonsense.

Until you have a sense of the damage to expect, resist buying a lot of expensive fish or water plants.

CHILDREN'S SAFETY 回回 A pond or even a fountain basin with a few inches of water in it poses a danger to young children. Unless you can always supervise your children or any child who visits your garden, build in safety features. A thick ring of plants around the water will delay a child reaching the water's edge, but the only safe barrier is a sturdy fence around that part of the garden, with a locked gate. The alternative is to fill the pond or low fountain basins with pebbles instead of water while children are young. Check local ordinances before building a pond that will be deeper than 18 inches; you may be required to put a fence around the water.

MOSQUITO CONTROL 回回 Mosquitoes breed in still water if there are no natural predators present. Control the larvae in one of three ways: introduce fish, which will eat the larvae; use a biological control; or, if you have a simple garden in a bowl or a bucket, tip the water out and replenish it every few days.

A few goldfish will consume all the mosquito larvae in the water. In a water bowl, consider a few tiny mosquito fish, available free in many parts of the United States from mosquito abatement agencies or county agricultural extension offices. The biological control is *B. t. israelensis;* it's available in small doughnuts or dunks that you float or crumble into the water. It's not harmful to fish.

WINTERIZING A WATER GARDEN 回回 Plans need to be made for fish, plants, and containers before winter starts. Even in a mild climate, an annual cleanup is beneficial, but don't go overboard and think about emptying out all the water, because you'll spoil the water quality and encourage algae.

Fall storms blow all kinds of leaves and debris into the water garden. Stretch netting over the water if there's a deciduous tree nearby. When all the leaves are down, go through the water carefully, sweeping, netting, or picking out the leaves before they start to decompose and damage the water quality.

Fish need less food during the winter; their metabolism changes, and they become less active. If you are feeding your fish regularly, reduce the feedings or, better still, stop feeding altogether until spring. Fish will survive cold winters provided there's an area of water that stays unfrozen at the bottom of the pond or container and there's a break in the surface ice so that gases toxic to the fish can escape. Don't smash the ice to make a hole, because the shock waves will kill the fish; rather, place a hot pan or a de-icer on the surface, and let the ice melt slowly. As long as the water is fairly clear of fish waste and decomposing organic matter, the cause of the gases, the fish can survive several days with no break in the ice. If the water will freeze completely solid, bring the fish indoors for the winter.

Many aquatic plants are hardy. They may die back to their roots, as lilies do in almost all climates, or sink to the bottom in clusters of overwintering buds, as water ferns do, but new shoots appear in spring. To keep the water clean, remove the dying foliage and prune away rotting stems and roots (keep the plants in a moist environment as you work, perhaps in a bucket or at least covered with wet newspaper); the more debris that's left to decompose in the water during winter, the greater the chance of a long algal bloom in spring, because the algae thrive on the nutrients released as the material rots. Where winters are harsh, place plant pots on the bottom of the pond; if the water is likely to freeze completely solid, remove the pots and overwinter the plants in a greenhouse pool or in the garage, wrapped in black plastic and kept moist all winter. Store nonhardy plants in the same way, except floaters, which do nicely in jars of water indoors.

Pumps can be run year-round unless the water will freeze solid, in which event, remove the pump indoors before the water freezes, and drain all the hoses. If ice forms and then melts, never freezing the whole pond, you can leave the pump in the water and run it during the warm periods to help aerate the water and generate oxygen for the fish. If you have a biofilter and the water may freeze, remove it, clean it, and restart it in spring.

Not all water bowls are frost-proof. If necessary, empty the bowls before the first frost, and bring them indoors. Or leave them outside, but turned upside-down so rainwater won't collect, freeze, and crack the bowl. Come spring, after the last frost, restock your water garden, and watch the lengthening days and warm weather bring out the water lily buds and the glisten on the water surface.

BASINS, BOWLS, AND JARS

Any watertight container—basin, bowl, urn, jar, dish, sink, concrete footing, hubcap—filled to the brim with water and placed along a path will stop people in their tracks. Put one where people will naturally pause: at the end of a path, at an intersection of two paths, beside a bench or an arch, at the front door. These might be the places for a large permanent water container, with an iris or gold and blue shubunkins. Small mobile containers might travel as needed, to cover a bare patch in the middle of a flower bed, to pull the eye away from an azalea gone brown, or more positively to mirror the potato vine just come into flower, and then move to another place in fall to catch the first tumbling blood red maple leaves. Drop a floating plant in one pot, to drift across the surface in a pretty pattern, covering and revealing the sky.

While you're looking for unusual watertight containers in salvage yards, look too for a column to place the container on. At eye height, the details come into view: the decoration on the outside of the bowl, the smooth or pocked interior, the skin of the water dusty with pollen.

Water containers placed on the ground, or sunk into it, attract wildlife. Spill water outside of the rim and butterflies may alight for a mud bath. Birds will land on the rim if they judge the area safe from predators, and then if the dish is shallow and not too smooth they'll splash about in the water.

WATER AND HERB PARTERRE

⌐⌐⌐⌐⌐⌐⌐⌐⌐⌐⌐⌐⌐⌐⌐⌐⌐⌐⌐⌐⌐⌐⌐⌐⌐⌐⌐⌐⌐⌐⌐⌐⌐

Wind sways the oaks on the edge of the garden and ripples in crosshatches across the eye of water in the warm herb-scented parterre. When the breeze stills at sunset, the sky swells pink and gold inside the rosy rim of the water bowl. Soon the dark tops of the oaks start to creep over the water. Then the light goes, leaving the water transparent, with garden dust and oak leaves floating on the surface.

HOW TO DO IT 回回

This bowl contains still water for reflections. The parterre plants make an embroidery pattern: a chain of green boxwood to mark the edge, a band of yellow buttons and long gray stitches of lavender cotton in the middle, and a center patch of gold-green glittery lemon thyme.

Choose a bowl that has a wide surface, to catch reflections. It need not be deep, because you can raise it on bricks. If the shape is pretty, the interior surface can be light in color, to show the contours of the bowl.

Mark out the parterre perimeter with the twine and stakes; make it 10 feet square. If you like, orient it within the garden as a diamond. Clear any weeds, till the soil to a depth of 8 inches, then rake it level.

Mark the center of the parterre, 5 feet from each edge. Firm the ground with your feet or the back of the spade, place the bricks in position, if necessary, and place the bowl on top of the bricks. Plan on growing the lemon thyme about 1 foot high to disguise the bricks. Check the rim of the bowl with the level to make sure that it's even.

Set out the plants in their pots on the soil surface, to get the pattern right before you start planting. Place the boxwood 6 inches inside the parterre boundary, 18 inches apart, five plants per side, plus one plant squarely at each corner of the parterre to keep the shape crisp. Place the lavender cotton 2 feet inside the boxwood, three per side, plus one squarely on each corner. Place the lemon thyme between the lavender cotton and the bowl, one set squarely on each corner.

Plant the plants in the ground, keeping the rows straight. Boxwood will grow faster and greener if you give it more water than the other plants, which prefer a dryish soil.

Fill the bowl with water to the very brim; a half-empty bowl has less reflection surface.

To keep mosquitoes from breeding in the bowl, sprinkle a biological control into the water.

Inexpensive
Easy
Location: Sun

Tools

Measuring tape
Twine and stakes
Spade or fork, for tilling
Rake
Level
Planting trowel
Hose or watering can

Ingredients

Bowl with wide surface
Bricks, to raise bowl, if necessary
24 boxwood (*Buxus* spp.)
16 lavender cotton (*Santolina chamaecyparissus*)
4 variegated lemon thyme (*Thymus citriodorus* 'Aureus')
Mosquito larvae control that contains *B. t. israelensis*

Maintenance

Top up water in bowl to keep it full to brim
Water plants regularly until established, then less frequently
Empty and scrub bowl clean every month
Replace mosquito control as necessary
Fertilize boxwood with a time-release fertilizer in spring
Clip boxwood twice a year, in early summer and late fall; when established, keep to 1 foot high
Shear lavender cotton hard after flowering; keep to 1 foot high
Pick tips of lemon thyme for kitchen; trim lightly in fall

RAIN DIMPLE AND FLOWERS

During a rain shower, water rushes over the surface of this rock, spilling into its elbows and dimples, and filling a shelf with a fresh clear pool. In the watery sunshine that follows, the pool reflects the clouds and the white silene flowers bent and dewy from the rain. Steam rises in the warm air, and the water evaporates slowly. A dusty skin settles on the shrinking surface. After the water is gone, the mineral salts and pine needles left behind start to crust into the layers and layers of old watermarks bleached into the stone.

HOW TO DO IT 回回 This rock contains ephemeral water from rain showers. It sits against a bank planted with silene and fairy wand. A rock this size is heavy; have someone help you drag, roll, and tip it into position, or ask the rock supplier whether the delivery person can install it.

Choose a rock that has a strong solid shape, good outlines on the sides that will be visible, and a surface with a large natural dimple at least 2 inches deep. The rock needs to be extra large to be convincing. A third of it will be buried below the soil surface, to appear natural.

Before the rock arrives, dig the hole for it. Make it one-third of the rock height.

Move the rock into position using a number of different tools, as necessary. You might move it on a platform (a sheet of plywood, or carpet if the rock has moss or algae that might get scratched) sitting atop three long poles that you can then use as rollers. Use a fourth pole to lever it on and off the platform. Or secure rope or chain around the rock, with carpet pads to help prevent scuffs, and drag it; tie a pole into the rope to turn the rock over. Once it's in the hole, a bar is useful to turn it into exactly the right place. Never try to lift a heavy rock; instead, raise it by rolling it up a plank set on an incline. Wear strong boots and gloves, and stand clear of the rock as you're moving it.

Once the rock is in position in the hole, backfill around it with soil, compacting the soil as you fill the hole.

Build a bank around the back of the rock, using soil from the hole and from another part of the garden. Firm the soil as you build the bank. Plant the silene on top of the bank, 18 inches apart. Plant the fairy wand 1 foot from the rock edge, so that its long grassy leaves and delicate flower stem will arch over the water. Plant the Cape fuchsia and hebe at the foot of the rock.

Moderately expensive
Moderately easy
Location: Sun

Tools
Spade, for digging
Tools for moving rock, such as plywood platform or carpet, 4 long poles, rope, chain, bar, plank for incline (see text)
Planting trowel
Hose or watering can

Ingredients
1 large rock with natural dimple
Silene *(Silene uniflora)*, approx. 9 per 1 square yard of bank
1 fairy wand *(Dierama pulcherrimum)*
1 Cape fuchsia *(Phygelius capensis)*
1 hebe, medium tall species

Maintenance
Water plants regularly

REFLECTION TUB,
CARVED HEADS, AND FERNS

In a hot entrance court, this generous tub of water sits under trees, catching the darkness and coolness of their shade. Black branches and black-green leaves pinpricked with spangles of light etch the water's silver skin. The tub is deep and shadowy, like the pools that hang under alder trees in a stream. Lying next to the water are two sleeping faces, tucked between emerald green ferns, cool and peaceful out of the sun.

HOW TO DO IT 🔲🔲

This tub contains still water for reflections and a few fish (optional).

Choose a tub that has a dark interior surface; that way the water will look black and mysterious. A light-colored interior will show the contours of the pot instead, and the scurfy watermarks and debris that collects on the bottom. A tub with an earthy-colored, scraped, or pocked exterior surface blends into the garden. A slick-surfaced, bright-colored, elegant tub will call more attention to itself.

Rake the ground level, and moisten it if it's dry. Make the tub stable by settling it firmly into the level wet soil. Start to fill the tub with water, then check the rim with the level to make sure that it's even. Fill the tub to the very brim; a half-empty bowl has less reflection surface.

Plant the ferns alongside the tub, in the shade.

Instead of carved heads, you could use any sculpture or pieces of natural material, such as driftwood or smooth river stones, that create a restful mood. Keep them small, so that the tub looks large in contrast to them.

To prevent a mosquito problem, place a few mosquito fish or goldfish in the water. Alternatively, use a biological control that contains *B. t. israelensis*. If you introduce fish into the tub, do not feed them; there's food enough in the water, and fish food will dirty the water.

Inexpensive
Easy
Location: Partial shade

Tools
Rake
Hose or watering can
Level
Planting trowel

Ingredients
Extra-large ceramic tub with dark interior surface
2 ferns (*Onoclea sensibilis* or any small fern)
Pieces of sculpture or other small objects
A few mosquito fish or goldfish, or mosquito larvae control that contains *B. t. israelensis*

Maintenance
Top up water in tub to keep it full to brim
Water ferns regularly
Replace fish or mosquito control as necessary
Empty and scrub tub clean every year

BIRDBATH IN A SHADE GARDEN

Here in Sharon Osmond's city garden, a salvaged birdbath sits below an evergreen ash. The robins come first to the lower branches of the ash, check the garden for cats, hop lower onto the lily-of-the-valley shrub, recheck, and then, if the sights are clear, descend into the birdbath. For a time every day, this old chipped ornament becomes as exciting as a waterfall: flashes of movement, splashing sounds, and water droplets spraying and glittering in the air. When the birds are gone and the water becomes still, dappled sunbeams wander across it, reflecting the sky into a quiet eye of light in the shade garden.

HOW TO DO IT ▧▧ This birdbath contains still, fresh water, for birds and reflections, and a floating aquatic plant, water pennywort, which some birds steal for nesting material.

Choose a natural-looking place for birds, with some shelter from wind. Rake the ground level, and moisten it if it's dry. Make the birdbath stable by settling it firmly into the level wet soil. Check the rim with the level to make sure that it's even. Fill the bowl with water to the very brim; a half-empty bowl has less reflection surface.

Drop the water pennywort into the bowl; it's an aquatic plant that thrives floating unrooted in water.

Plant the lily-of-the-valley shrub behind the birdbath, about 18 inches from the base. Plant the ivy close to the base, and when a stem grows long enough, twine it around the pedestal. Fill in around the birdbath with any shade-loving medium-height plants. The objective is to have the foliage mask the base so that your eye is drawn to the sparkling water in the bowl rather than to the birdbath's silhouette.

As the pennywort grows, remove parts of it to keep most of the water surface clear and reflecting light. Because birds love fresh water, refill the bowl frequently, as often as daily. If there's an irrigation line nearby, clip an emitter to the back of the bowl.

Inexpensive
Easy
Location: Partial shade

Tools
Rake
Hose or watering can
Level
Planting trowel

Ingredients
Stone or concrete birdbath
1 water pennywort (*Hydrocotyle vulgaris*) or other floating aquatic plant
1 lily-of-the-valley shrub (*Pieris japonica*)
1 variegated ivy (*Hedera canariensis* 'Variegata,' or any variegated ivy)
Shade-loving medium-height foliage plants to fill in area
Irrigation line emitter (optional)

Maintenance
Replace water in birdbath frequently to attract birds
Water plants regularly
Fertilize lily-of-the-valley shrub regularly with formula for acid-loving plants
Remove pieces of pennywort as it spreads
Empty and scrub birdbath basin clean every few months
Replace pennywort in spring, after last frost

WATER JAR WITH IRISES

At eye level in a jar of clear water, buds of Japanese water irises unfold one by one during spring. They slip out of their sheaths, tips of fresh violet blue among the green and cream leaves. Then the falls untwist, and the standards peel away. Within the hour, the standards have taken their upright positions and the falls are somersaulting back over the sheath, forming 4-inch blue saucers rippled with white and gold. If you stir the water, the floating water fern will bob toward the rim and up the bases of the sedges, leaving a wake of sparkling water and irises reflected against the sky.

HOW TO DO IT 回回

This jar contains still water, aquatic plants, and a few fish (optional). The plants sit on a submerged tray that's hooked onto the rim of the jar.

Choose a large jar or pot with a wide top and a distinct rim onto which you can hook the plant tray. This jar is 20 inches across at the rim, and 28 inches tall, plus a few extra inches because it's raised onto a concrete-paver base. Place the jar as a single focal point, or as a centerpiece in a collection of smaller pots.

Set up the nail hooks and plant tray: Bend each nail into a large C. Hook them over the rim onto the outside of the jar and back under the neck of the jar. Attach wire to the tray edge in three places. Place the tray inside the jar, and loop the wire over the nail hooks, twisting it round itself until it's secure. When the tray feels sturdy, place the deepest plant pot on the tray. Readjust the length of the wires so that the top of that plant pot will be just below the water surface when the jar is filled to the brim.

When you have the tray suspended correctly, place the other plants on the tray; elevate any shallow pots on flat pebbles or a brick. Fill the jar with water.

Drop the water fern onto the surface. It will float, unrooted, and help keep the water clear.

To deter raccoons, place the saw blades around the jar rim, under the hooks (optional). To prevent a mosquito problem, place a few mosquito fish or goldfish in the water. Alternatively, use a biological control that contains *B. t. israelensis*. If you introduce fish into the tub, do not feed them; there's food enough in the water, and fish food will dirty the water.

Inexpensive
Easy
Location: Sun

Tools
Pliers, to bend nails into hooks and cut wire
Hose or watering can

Ingredients
Large jar with wide (20-inch) mouth and distinct rim
Concrete pavers, to raise jar (optional)
1 white and purple-blue Japanese water iris (*Iris laevigata* 'Albopurpurea colchesterensis,' or similar variety)
1 purple-blue variegated Japanese water iris (*Iris laevigata* 'Variegata')
2 small water-loving sedges (*Kyllingia* or *Dichromena*)
3 nails, 6 inches long
Thick wire
Tray, such as a circular wire plant support, largest diameter that will fit through neck of jar
Pebbles or bricks, to raise shallow pots on tray, if necessary
Water fern (*Azolla*), 1 scoop
3 saw blades, for rim, to deter raccoons (optional)
A few mosquito fish or goldfish, or mosquito larvae control that contains *B. t. israelensis*

Maintenance
Top up water in jar frequently
Replace fish or mosquito control as necessary
Thin water fern when it gets crowded; in cold-winter areas, replace it in spring if necessary
Fertilize plants with slow-release pellets in spring
Divide irises every 3 years

PAIR OF WATER POTS:
ONE LILY, ONE FERN

A sedum and a geranium have grown up around the pots, flourishing in the moist soil where the water sometimes spills. Their rose pink flowers—geranium in spring and summer, sedum in fall—highlight the pink on the rim of the tall pot and the burnished pink of the water fern when the weather turns cool.

The Comanche water lily buds are cream when they open; as they mature they turn peachy pink with flecks of orange. The lily is a small refined "changeable" kind but has a large pot to itself, so that the maroon-speckled pads can spread loosely on the open water.

HOW TO DO IT 回回

One pot holds the water lily, planted in a container. The other pot contains floating water fern.

Choose two pots of different heights. Water lilies look especially lovely in pots with very wide rims. The water lily pot shown in the photograph is 33 inches across at the rim and 20 inches high. The tall pot is 18 inches across at the rim and 28 inches high. Place the pots close together. Raise the lily pot on the concrete pavers or bricks (optional).

Choose a water lily in the small category. Avoid varieties that need more than 15 inches of water over the crowns. If your pot will receive less than six hours of full sun each day, select a variety that tolerates some shade. Raised in a pot, the lily's flowers and leaves can be inspected up close, so consider fragrance and colors of leaves and flower stamens. When Comanche opens, its stamens are bright gold; the flowers are lightly fragrant.

With the hose, fill the water pot for the lily to within 4 inches of the rim. Place four bricks on the bottom to support the lily container.

Plant the lily into the 12-inch plastic container. Fill the container with plain unimproved garden soil, not potting soil. The crown (where the stems meet the tuber) must be just above the soil surface.

Push the lily fertilizer pellets into the soil, according to the instructions on the label. Place the gravel over the soil surface, to prevent the soil from floating into the water. Water the container until it's completely waterlogged.

Place the lily container into the water pot. Gently fill the pot with water to the rim.

Fill the tall pot with water. Drop the water fern onto the surface. It will float, unrooted, and help keep the water clear. Place the glass ball on the water.

To prevent a mosquito problem, place a few mosquito fish or two small goldfish in each pot. Alternatively, use a biological control that contains *B. t. israelensis*. If you introduce fish into the pots, do not feed them; there's food enough in the water, and fish food will dirty the water.

Plant the sedum and geranium at the base of the pots.

Inexpensive
Easy
Location: Sun or partial shade

Tools
Hose or watering can
Planting trowel

Ingredients
Wide-rimmed water pot for lily, frost-proof if necessary
Tall water pot for fern, frost-proof if necessary
Concrete pavers or bricks, to raise either pot (optional)
1 water lily that doesn't need deep water, such as *Nymphaea* 'Comanche' or a smaller variety
4 to 6 bricks, to support lily container
Shallow 12-inch pot for lily, solid black plastic or perforated
Garden soil
Fertilizer pellets formulated for lilies
Gravel, rinsed, several handfuls
Water fern *(Azolla)*, 1 scoop
1 glass ball
A few mosquito fish or 4 small goldfish, or mosquito larvae control that contains *B. t. israelensis*
1 sedum (*Sedum telephium* 'Autumn Joy')
1 geranium (*Geranium oxonianum* 'Rose Clair')

Maintenance
Top up water in pots frequently
Water sedum and geranium regularly
Remove bricks under lily container as lily stems grow
Feed lily regularly, as recommended
Remove dead leaves, stems, and flowers from pots regularly
Thin water fern when it gets crowded; in cold-winter areas, replace it in spring if necessary

FOUNTAINS

Jets hiss cool silver spumes up into the air. The water flies in the light then falls in breaking beads into the catchment basin, spitting against the waves lapping toward the rim.

Moving water also murmurs, slaps, chuckles, burbles, plops, pitter-patters. The sound changes with the wind: when a chute in a free fall is flung off course for a moment, there's silence, then water dripping down through foliage alongside the regular splashing off the back plate. The sounds soothe like rain or wind on a windowpane, overwriting the noise of traffic.

Listen to the sounds a fountain makes before you decide on it. Does the water make just one sound, tipping in a straight chute, like a faucet, from spout to trough, or does it splash against stone on the way down, or echo first through a bamboo spout, or lap around a scalloped basin, or three basins? The sound can be quite complex and musical. Consider how wind might affect the sound, where the spray will blow in your garden, whether cool spray will create a chilly or a refreshing place.

Think also how the water will catch light. Water swilling about in a sunlit basin appears as a dazzle of light shards from one viewpoint; from another you can see sunbeams wobbling through the surface and flickering against the underwater stone. Backlit, a spray of water makes an arc of crystals, an especially striking display against a plain green backdrop.

On the way down, water can accent an interesting surface. Aluminum tanks and copper piping gleam when wet, pebbles reveal their grain and earth colors, ceramic glazes shine; droplets sliding over leaves and flowers make them tremble and leave them clean.

The sound of moving water or the sight of a plume of spray rising above a hedge will lure people out into the garden or deeper into the garden. Maybe the fountain is the destination if it's a piece of art that celebrates the movement and sight of water, or if it's a gargoyle spitting from a back plate into a sunny trough, with a bench right alongside in the shade. Maybe the fountain is merely beside the path, a moment's stopping place now that the gazebo has come into view.

All fountains contain a pump, which needs an electrical supply. The pumps are usually small ones submerged in the catchment basin, hidden beneath a stone; they make no noise. The electrical cable is hidden in the fountain base or slipped out over the side of a bowl or liner basin, camouflaged by an overhanging leaf or a rock. See pages 35–37 and 38–39 for more information about pumps and outdoor electricity.

BUBBLING ROCK POOL

A spring gurgles underneath the rocks. As it comes to the surface, it sends rivulets of waves across the pool, against the sides of the sun-warmed rocks, and out over the rim. The spill wets the surrounding boulders, then drips back underground, through the cool shade. Moisture-loving rush and plantain grow in the splash zone. At noon the garden bakes in a still heat, to the tune of crystal clear, cool water bubbling up from the ground.

HOW TO DO IT 回回

This fountain contains a small submersible pump in a PVC-lined catchment basin below the water bowl. Water is circulated through a plastic tube from the pump up through a hole in the bowl to the water surface. Before you begin, check that the electrical cable on the pump will reach a GFI outlet nearby. If necessary, order a pump with a longer cable, or have a GFI outlet installed by an electrician. Also, before you purchase the bowl, check that the rim is perfectly level so the water will spill over it on all sides.

To make the catchment basin, dig a hole 2½ feet across and 12 inches deep. Remove any sharp stones or roots from the bottom and sides of the hole. Firm the soil.

Place the liner underlayment into the hole. Trim the corners, and keep the trimmings. Lay the liner on top of the underlayment.

To protect the liner, put underlayment trimmings on it where the water bowl will go. Place the concrete blocks on the trimmings, about 1 foot apart, to support the bowl.

Place a flat rock outside one of the concrete blocks, and sit the pump on it. The pump needs to be off the liner so that it doesn't become clogged with sediment. To protect the pump further, and reduce maintenance, see page 38. Note the positions of the flow adjuster on the pump and of the water intake. Lay the electrical cable across the top of the liner, in the direction of the GFI outlet.

Drill a ½-inch hole in the base of the water bowl, if it doesn't have one, for the plastic tubing. Set the water bowl on top of the concrete blocks, and use the level to check that it's perfectly even. If it's off kilter, the water will spill over only one part of the rim.

Push one end of the plastic tubing over the outlet on the pump. Thread the tubing around or through the center of one concrete block and up through the hole into the water bowl. Caulk around the tubing at the hole, to make the bowl watertight.

Arrange rocks on the liner around the bowl. Leave space below the rim so the water will drip into the catchment basin and not roll over the rocks and evaporate. Save the rocks that have the prettiest shapes and colors when wet for the inside of the water bowl.

Moderately inexpensive
Moderately easy
Location: Sun or partial shade

Tools

Spade, for digging
Pruning shears or knife, to remove roots if necessary
Scissors
Drill with ½-inch masonry bit, if bowl has no drainage hole
Level
Spatula or knife, for applying caulking
Hose or watering can
Planting trowel

Ingredients

Pond liner underlayment, 4 by 4 feet; or use old carpet or newspapers
Black pond liner, 5 by 5 feet, PVC or butyl or EPDM, 30 to 45 mil
2 small concrete blocks, to support water bowl
Rocks and pebbles, river-washed, interesting shapes and colors, some flat, approx. ½ wheelbarrowful
Submersible pump, 180 GPH, with flow adjuster
Water bowl, 20 inches in diameter, approx. 9 inches deep, with absolutely level rim, with or without drainage hole, frost-proof if necessary
Plastic tubing, 2 feet long, flexible but thick-walled, diameter to fit pump outlet
Silicon caulking
1 rush (*Juncus* spp.)
1 water plantain (*Plantago major* 'Atropurpurea')
1 euphorbia (*Euphorbia dulcis* 'Chameleon')
1 variegated sedum (*Sedum alboroseum* 'Medio-Variegata')
Mosquito larvae control that contains *B. t. israelensis*

Maintenance

Refill catchment basin regularly
Water plants regularly
Replace mosquito control as necessary
Keep pump intake clear
In severe winters, remove pump before water freezes

Trim the corners of the liner, and bury the edges. Spread pebbles where patches of liner show. Slip the electricity cable behind the rocks.

When the caulking is dry, finish the water bowl. Arrange five or six rocks in the bowl. Lay a flat one across two others to make a bridge; the bridge should be higher than the rim of the bowl. Fit the elbow onto the plastic tubing, and place it under the bridge so that it sits about 1 inch below the water surface when the bowl is filled.

Fill the catchment basin and water bowl with water. Plug the electrical cable into the GFI outlet, and turn the fountain on. Adjust the water flow, and rearrange the rocks and the tubing until you like the sound of the water bubbling and spilling.

Plant the plants in the soil beyond the liner.

To prevent a mosquito problem, use a biological control that contains *B. t. israelensis.*

GARGOYLE BACK PLATE AND TROUGH

The gargoyle spews water into a small basin, splashing green waves up against the back plate. The water eddies, then spills over the lip in another free fall, to the trough. Here, as it grows still, its murmurs echo in a grotto of collected silt, trumpet creeper petals, and tide-marks.

In a breeze, the tips of the vine bounce over the fountain, and the water chute curls off course. Spray drips down the sides of the basin and the trough, filling dozens of pockets worn into the surfaces. In these puddles, ferns germinate and spore, a daisy seedling sprouts.

HOW TO DO IT 回回 This fountain is composed of a Mexican stone trough and a back plate, which sits on the trough edge. A submersible pump in an alcove at the back of the trough pumps water through plastic tubing behind the back plate up to the gargoyle. Before you begin, check that the electrical cable on the pump will reach a GFI outlet nearby. If necessary, order a pump with a longer cable, or have a GFI outlet installed by an electrician. Ask friends to help you lift the trough and back plate into position.

Choose a location in front of a wall or fence. Put on sturdy boots and gloves and build a dry-laid wall base for the trough. Place the large corner-stones first. Make the wall two stones wide, placing occasional long "stretcher" stones across the two piles for stability. Start each course at the corners and work toward the center, laying the stones flattest side down, canting them inward for stability, and filling between them with small stones and chips. The top of the trough needs to be at least 2 feet off the ground, so people don't have to stoop to touch the water. Be sure the base is stable.

Lift the trough onto the base. Use the level to check that it's perfectly evenly settled. If it's off kilter, the water will look lower on one end or side of the trough than the other, a very jarring perception. Once the trough is full, it will be too heavy to move. Check that the wall rocks are still stable.

Put a flat stone chip inside the alcove, and sit the pump on it. The pump needs to be off the bottom so that it doesn't become clogged with sediment. Push one end of the plastic tubing over the outlet on the pump. Lay the electrical cable over the top of the trough and along the back of it toward the GFI outlet. Note the positions of the flow adjuster on the pump and of the water intake.

Place the back plate on the edge of the trough. Holding the plate steady, take the plastic tubing up the back of it and push it into the gargoyle. The back plate is so heavy, gravity should hold it in place; be sure there's no danger of it sliding or toppling.

Fill the trough to the rim. Plug the electrical cable into a GFI outlet, and turn it on. Listen to the sound of the water from different points in the garden; if necessary, adjust the flow on the pump or place a rock in the trough.

Plant the vine 1½ feet from the trough. In summer, hummingbirds will visit the fountain, to feed on the nectar in the trumpet creeper flowers and to drink from the water's edge. Mosses will quickly take hold in the pocked stone.

Moderately expensive
Moderately easy
Location: Sun or partial shade

Tools
Measuring tape
Level
Hose or watering can
Spade, for planting vine

Ingredients
Wall rock, flat-sided, for fountain base, including cornerstones, stretcher stones, and chips
Stone trough and back plate
Submersible pump, 140 GPH, with flow adjuster
Plastic tubing, 3 feet long, flexible but thick-walled, diameter to fit pump outlet
1 trumpet creeper (*Campsis* spp.)

Maintenance
Refill trough regularly
Water vine regularly
Keep pump intake clear
In severe winters, remove pump before water freezes

THREE-TIERED
ITALIAN FOUNTAIN

As water slaps from basin to basin, a warm breeze pulls away some of its coolness, refreshing the air in a hot entrance garden. On still days, the moist air mixes with the perfume of the roses and lavender on the banks and the thyme in the cracks in the floor. The garden is soft-edged but formal: the fountain sits dead center in a broad path that arrives straight as an arrow at a pair of grand columns on the porch.

HOW TO DO IT 🔲🔲

This concrete fountain comes in the form of a kit. A submersible pump inside the pedestal at the bottom of the lowest basin pumps water through plastic tubing in the pedestal to the top of the fountain. Before you begin, check that the electrical cable on the pump will reach a GFI outlet nearby. If necessary, order a pump with a longer cable, or have a GFI outlet installed by an electrician. Ask a friend or two to help you lift the basins into position. Be very careful that children do not climb on this fountain or adults lean against it; it may topple.

Choose a position for the fountain that aligns with something architectural in the garden, such as a pair of benches, an arbor, a gate, or french windows. A courtyard is also a fine place for this fountain or a corner garden where two high walls meet. The ground must be firm in all weather; if rain makes the base soft, the fountain may topple. In questionable situations, consider laying paving on a deep base below the fountain or installing a concrete pad.

Clear the site, and use the level to check that the ground is even. Mark the position for the fountain with construction chalk, measuring off the distances from the benches or walls carefully; a small misalignment will show. If you're working in a paved area, spread padding under the fountain pieces; if you jolt them against a hard surface, they may chip.

Follow the kit instructions, placing the pump in the pedestal, the plastic tubing over the pump outlet, and the electrical cable out underneath the bottom of the pedestal toward the GFI outlet. Note the positions of the flow adjuster on the pump and of the water intake.

Each upper piece of the fountain rests on top of another, the tubing runs through the center of each piece, and the whole unit holds together by gravity. To be stable, each piece must be centered carefully and the basins made level. If a basin won't rest level on the pedestal piece below, wedge a thin wood chip between the two to raise one side of the basin. Don't glue or mortar the pieces together, because you may need to dismantle the fountain at some point.

Fill the basins to the rim. Plug the electrical cable into the GFI outlet, and turn it on. Listen to the sound of the water from different points in the garden; if necessary, adjust the flow on the pump or trim the tube in the top of the fountain—the lower it is in the fountain, the gentler the flow will be.

Plant the daylilies around the fountain base, 1½ feet apart, 1 foot from the

Moderately expensive
Moderately easy
Location: Sun

Tools
Level
Construction chalk
Measuring tape
Padding for work area, if necessary
Hose or watering can
Spade and trowel, for planting
Plastic tubing, to siphon out water in
    winter, if necessary

Ingredients
1 fountain kit, including 300- to 500-GPH
    pump, tubing, pedestals, and basins
Thin wood chips, 1 handful, for balancing
    basins, if necessary
6 daylilies (Hemerocallis 'Stella d'Oro'), for
    fountain base
Thyme (Thymus pseudolanuginosus), 2 per
    1 foot of paving cracks if appropriate
Lavenders (Lavandula angustifolia), approx.
    1 per 1 square yard
Roses (Rosa 'Iceberg'), approx. 1 per
    1 square yard

Maintenance
Refill bowls regularly
Water plants regularly
Scrub basins clean as necessary with
    stiff brush
Drain fountain completely to protect
    against frost damage

pedestal. Plant the thyme 6 inches apart between paving stones or bricks, if appropriate. Plant the lavenders in a sweep, 2½ feet apart, and the roses 2 feet behind them, 3 feet apart.

In winter, be careful not to leave water standing in the bowls if it might freeze, because the concrete may crack. Use the drain plug to empty the bottom basin, and siphon the water from the upper bowls with a length of plastic tubing.

BAMBOO GROVE
AND WATERSPOUT

A stand of giant bamboo high above and around the waterspout rustles in every gust of wind. At the height of each spate of shivering, the splash from the spout is blown higher up the rock, and the green glass ball is set drifting across the water surface, which flickers madly with light and shadow. In quiet moments, the water patters on the large sunny rock, bounces off its sides onto smaller rocks, drawing out their bright colors in the water stain, and drips down to the pool. The glass ball hangs still against the rim, reflecting the water surface reflecting the tips of the bamboo.

HOW TO DO IT 回回

This fountain contains a small submersible pump inside the water bowl. Water is circulated through a plastic tube from the pump up the bamboo and into the spout. Before you begin, check that the electrical cable on the pump will reach a GFI outlet nearby. If necessary, order a pump with a longer cable, or have a GFI outlet installed by an electrician.

Saw the bamboo pole into three lengths: one 30 inches, one 36 inches, one 42 inches. Make the cuts ½ inch above a node (a ring around the pole), through the corky membrane that blocks the hollow bamboo at each node. The membrane makes an interesting top to the bamboo pieces.

Take the 36-inch length of bamboo for the fountain piece. To prepare it for the plastic tubing, drill a 1-inch hole through the center of each layer of membrane, starting at the bottom of the pole. Use the extension piece on the drill to reach into the interior of the pole. If necessary, drill through the top of the pole to reach the node below it; fill this hole later with a cork. (If you don't have a drill extension, try to break through the membranes with a stake, working from the bottom of the pole and leaving the membrane at the top of the pole intact.)

Make a hole for the waterspout by drilling a 1-inch hole 4 inches from the top of the bamboo. Drop one end of the chain through the spout hole, and shake it down through and out the bottom of the bamboo. Pry open the last link in the chain, and pierce the plastic tubing with it so that chain and tube are firmly attached. Pull on the other end of the chain, threading the tubing up through the bamboo and out through the spout hole. Fit the metal spout over the tubing and push it into the bamboo at an angle. Check that the tubing is not crimped. Once you have the tubing in place, remove the chain.

Place the water bowl in position. Put a large flat pebble inside, and sit the pump on it. The pump needs to be off the bottom so that it doesn't become clogged with sediment. To protect the pump further, and reduce maintenance, see page 38.

Move the bamboo piece with the tubing into the bowl; place it toward the far side of the bowl. Push the end of the plastic tubing at the bottom of the bamboo over the outlet on the pump. Wedge the bamboo upright with stones around the base. Lay the electrical cable over the rim on the far side of the bowl. Note the positions of the flow adjuster on the pump and of the water intake.

Moderately inexpensive
Moderately easy
Location: Sun or partial shade

Tools

Hacksaw
Drill with 1-inch bit and 18- or 24-inch extension piece (or stake instead of extension piece)
Chain, minimum 4 feet long, with small links, to thread through spout hole
Hose or watering can
Level
Spade
Planting trowel

Ingredients

Bamboo pole, 9 feet long, 4 inches in diameter
Cork, 1 inch in diameter, to fill drilling hole, if necessary
Plastic tubing, 3 feet long, flexible but thick-walled, diameter to fit pump outlet, smaller than spout diameter
Metal spout, rusty iron or new copper pipe, 6 inches long, 1 inch in diameter
Water bowl, approx. 22 inches in diameter, 18 inches deep, frost-proof if necessary
Submersible pump, 180 GPH, with flow adjuster
Pebbles, large and small, colorful river-washed kind, such as Pamy pebbles, 1 bucketful
8 or 9 river-washed stones, 10 to 15 inches across, interesting shapes and colors
Clip to reduce water flow (optional)
Gravel, colorful river-washed kind, such as Salmon Bay gravel, 1 bucketful
2 glass balls
Bamboo, clumping kind, approx. 1 per 6 square feet
1 variegated elderberry (*Sambucus nigra* 'Variegata')
1 Mexican feather grass (*Stipa tenuissima*)
Mosquito larvae control that contains *B. t. israelensis*

Maintenance

Refill bowl regularly
Water plants regularly
Keep pump intake clear
Replace mosquito control as necessary
In severe winters, remove pump before water freezes

Stack three or four large stones in the water bowl. Move them around until two break the surface and create a bay in the foreground. Haul the largest stone up over the rim of the bowl; it will take the eye away from the shape of the rim.

Start to fill the bowl with water. When it's one-quarter full, use the level to check that the bowl is settled perfectly evenly. If it's off kilter, the water will look lower on one side of the bowl than the other, a very jarring perception. Once the bowl is full, it will be too heavy to move.

Fill the bowl to within a few inches of the rim. Plug the electrical cable into a GFI outlet, and turn it on. Adjust the water flow on the pump, the angle of the waterspout, and the positions of the stones until the water splashes off one stone before it hits the surface in the bowl. Listen to the sound from different points in the garden; if necessary, position pebbles in the flow of the water to break too harsh a splash. (If you can't get the sound gentle enough, even at the lowest flow, you can pinch the tubing a little, with a clip, to reduce the flow, but the pump will be strained if you block more than 25 percent of the flow.) Create a beach on the near side of the bowl with pebbles and gravel. Leave the far side of the bowl free of pebbles, so the water seems to flow out from the bay, through a channel between the rocks, into the deep.

Fill the bowl to the brim. Float one of the glass balls on the water surface. Arrange gravel on the rim of the near side of the bowl, as if it were washed there. As a last step, double-check that the pump intake is not blocked and that the plastic tubing is not kinked.

Position the other two pieces of bamboo behind the bowl. Dig 8-inch-deep holes for them, and pack the soil back against them until they're firm. On the ground on the near side of the bowl, place three large stones, the rest of the pebbles and gravel, and the second glass ball. Replicating these decorative elements inside and outside of the bowl settles the water feature beautifully into its site.

Plant the plants around the bowl. Place the bamboo and elderberry 2 to 3 feet back from the bowl, the grass about 1½ feet away. Because all the plant leaves are small, light will flicker through them onto the water and cast lovely shadows on the outside of the bowl, softening the shape of it.

To keep mosquitoes from breeding in the bowl, sprinkle a biological control into the water.

DARK TUB, SCARLET BLOSSOMS, AND GOLDFISH

The water sits in a corner of a hot dry city courtyard, dark and cool in the jungle shade of banana leaves and fragrant nicotianas and ginger lilies. Scarlet blossoms drift on the shadowy surface, and bright goldfish flash in and out of the darkness.

A gurgle of water springs from an underwater pipe in the tub. It echoes against the walls and crosses the courtyard, where emerald baby's tears soak up the moisture between the bricks, and brilliant pink and red busy lizzies and fuchsias flower almost nonstop under a tropical ceiling of tree ferns.

HOW TO DO IT 回回
A small submersible pump sits inside the plastic tub. Water bubbles up from a plastic tube held below the surface between rocks. Before you begin, check that the electrical cable on the pump will reach a GFI outlet nearby. If necessary, order a pump with a longer cable, or have a GFI outlet installed by an electrician.

Place the water tub in position. Put one brick inside the tub, and sit the pump on it. The pump needs to be off the bottom so that it doesn't become clogged with sediment. To protect the pump further, and reduce maintenance, see page 38.

Push one end of the plastic tubing over the outlet on the pump. Lay the electrical cable over the rim on the far side of the tub. Note the positions of the flow adjuster on the pump and of the water intake.

Place one concrete block on each side of the pump. Place the rocks on the blocks; use bricks to raise the rocks so they will break the water surface, if you like. Wedge the tubing from the pump between the rocks. Leave the top of the tubing about 1 inch below the surface for a gentle gurgle. If the tubing won't stay upright, wire it to the rocks.

Start to fill the tub with water. When it's one-quarter full, use the level to check that it's settled perfectly evenly. If it's off kilter, the water will look lower on one side of the tub than the other, a very jarring perception. Once the tub is full, it will be too heavy to move.

Fill the tub to the brim. Plug the electrical cable into a GFI outlet. Adjust the water flow on the pump and the angle of the tubing until the sound is pleasing. If you like, bring the top of the tubing to the surface, and have the jet splash onto the stones. Place the moss around the tubing to disguise it.

Plant the plants around the tub in rich organic soil (amend the soil if necessary). Plant one or two nicotianas in front of the tub. Plant the banana tree in a sheltered spot, out of wind, at least 1½ feet from the tub. Plant the tree ferns 6 feet from the banana tree and each other. Plant the Chinese bellflower 2 to 4 feet from the tub, and let it ramble, vinelike, up a trellis or through the fuchsias and ginger lilies, planted 3 feet apart. Fill in with busy lizzies and the rest of the nicotianas.

Introduce the goldfish a week or two after filling the tub. Float the bag of fish on the water surface for 20 minutes before releasing the fish. The water will stay quite clear and the goldfish will thrive if you have only a couple and you do not feed them. Feeding the fish regularly will foul the water.

Inexpensive
Easy
Location: Sun or partial shade

Tools
Hose or watering can
Level
Planting trowel

Ingredients
Water tub, dark brown or black plastic, approx. 24 inches tall, 30 inches in diameter
Bricks, 1 to support pump and 6 to support rocks, if necessary
Submersible pump, 80 GPH, with flow adjuster
Plastic tubing, 2 feet long, diameter to fit pump outlet
2 concrete blocks, to support rocks
2 large rocks, craggy or river-washed, at least 10 inches in diameter
Wire, to hold tubing upright, if necessary
Moss, 1 sheet (optional)
6 nicotianas (Nicotiana alata or N. sylvestris), 1 small cell-pack
1 banana tree (Musa or Ensete spp.)
2 tree ferns (Cyathea cooperi)
1 Chinese bellflower (Abutilon hybridum, red flowering variety)
2 or 3 fuchsias, tall showy hybrids in vivid colors
2 or 3 ginger lilies (Hedychium spp.)
6 busy lizzies (Impatiens spp., vivid colors), 1 small cell-pack
2 goldfish

Maintenance
Refill tub regularly
Water and fertilize plants frequently
Keep pump intake clear
Watch for whitefly on fuchsias and bellflower; use soap solution
Pinch out tips of fuchsias and bellflower if plants get rangy
Once a year, remove goldfish and replace *half* of water

PONDS

A pond holds a generous amount of water. Expect herons to check it out — even if it's a 6-by-10-foot preformed shell — and mist to form on it. Wind will shuffle up ripples at one end, while water at the opposite bank stays calm. A pond has space enough for glittering channels of open sunny water and also dark places, where shadows play across the silty bottom. Leaves will blow in: thin willow blades, rough sycamore hands, birch hearts, fir needles. After a storm you're likely to find floating among them rose pink blossoms from someone's trumpet vine.

A pond can be left as plainly decorated as that. The water is on display then, and it's ornament enough. Even on a drizzly day, a pond is beautiful; water plops softly into the gray wash and keeps on dripping from the bank after the rain has stopped. There's always a skin of pollen and petals or sap from the pine, or a water spider, or a brief bloom of pea green algae, or metallic red and blue dragonflies mating.

You might add a fountain or waterfall for the sound of a splash or trickle or to help oxygenate the water for fish. Fish add color to the water, but more than that they make tracks through a watery world we can't reach — the cool undersides of the banks, the spawning places in emerald pondweeds.

The seaweedy submerged plants, oxygenators, help keep the water clear by absorbing nutrients from fish waste and decomposing leaves, so make them the first plants on your plant list. The rest of the list can run out of hand: a water lily for its dark buds unfolding into gold-centered bobbing cups, and also for its pads that roll open from tubes and then fill with dew and splash; bold plantain and arrowhead, for their sharp long tropical shadows and their leaf undersides high above the pond, which catch wobbling light reflected off the water surface; a variety of floaters — water pennywort, water fern, water clover — for their patterns; or a stand of reeds for their long romantic reflections.

Simple ponds are simple to build and maintain. Ponds with everything are the most ambitious water features you can choose. They are elaborate other worlds in miniature. If you can find the time to watch the small events of nature mirrored there each day, you'll have no trouble attending occasionally to the pump and the filter and the experimental business of balancing water clarity against fish numbers and plant growth. For more information on pond management, see pages 31–33 and 35–38.

REFLECTION POND WITH CHERUB

Three unobtrusive stepping-stones from a terrace with a city view, this green pond hides behind a curtain of clematis vines in a space the size of a compost heap. Marjory Harris weeds her main garden all summer and lights it at twilight for company; here in her secret garden, the algae sometimes bloom unhindered in a pea green cloud that conceals the bottom of the pond and rings the edges with velvety tidemarks.

It's hard to tell when anyone last came here, because the foxgloves and love-in-a-mist have seeded themselves along the path, and the trellis has rusted among the vines. The dusty shadow of the sculpture shimmers unobserved in the idle water. Black damselflies might hover here—no one would know.

HOW TO DO IT 回回 This is a simple reflection pond, edged with mortared brick. It is easily made with a black pond shell (designer Harland Hand made it in concrete).

Clear a level area for the pond. For a 3-by-5-foot pond shell, dig a trench 4 feet wide, 6 feet long, and 3 inches deeper than the shell. Remove the soil to another area of the garden; the ground surrounding the pond should be level or fall away a little, to prevent runoff into the pond.

Use the level—for the long edges, place it atop the piece of two-by-four— to ensure that the pond edges are perfectly level; when the pond is filled, the waterline will draw attention to even a slight slope. Remove any rocks, and firm the bottom of the trench.

Moisten the sand in the wheelbarrow. Spread a 3-inch layer into the bottom of the trench. Smooth and firm it.

Lower the shell into the trench, and adjust it until the rim sits at soil height and the shell is perfectly level. If necessary, remove the shell to rework the bottom of the trench. When the shell sits perfectly level, begin trickling water into it from the hose. At the same time, begin backfilling the space around the shell with sand, firming it with the small piece of two-by-four. Borrow the hose to water the sand, and firm it again to remove air pockets. Backfill around the shell to 4 inches or so, check that the pond is settling perfectly level, then keep backfilling a little ahead of the water level in the shell.

Wet the bricks thoroughly, and leave them for two hours. Level and compact the sand and soil around the pond. When the bricks are ready, mix about ½ cubic foot of mortar in the wheelbarrow, following the directions on the bag. It should spread easily but not run.

With the trowel, scoop mortar in a 6-inch-wide, ½-inch-thick strip along one short edge of the pond. Keep the mortar out of the water; the lime in it will destroy the water quality. Jab stipples along the strip with the point of the trowel. Place the bricks in a basketweave pattern, as shown in the photograph, leaving roughly ½-inch joints between them, the bricks overlapping the pond edge by 1 inch. Tap each brick into the mortar with the hammer handle. With the level, check that they are flat. Work around the pond, laying the bricks but leaving the joints empty. Clean the tools before the mortar sets.

Wait twenty-four hours before grouting the joints. Mix a small batch of fresh mortar, and use the trowel to pack it into the joints. Wipe stray mortar

Moderately inexpensive
Moderately easy
Location: Sun or light shade

Tools
Measuring tape
Straight-edged spade, for digging
Wheelbarrow
Level
Straight piece of two-by-four, 7 feet long
Hose
Piece of two-by-four, 1 foot long
Builder's trowel, pointed
Hammer
Cloth, for scrubbing bricks
Vinegar
Plastic sheet, 4 by 6 feet
Planting trowel

Ingredients
Pond shell, high-quality, black, 3 by 5 feet
Builder's sand, approx. ¾ cubic yard
60 bricks, old or rough for rustic character
Ready-mix mortar
Cherub
6 foxgloves (Digitalis purpurea)
12 love-in-a-mist (Nigella damascena),
    2 small cell-packs

Maintenance
Water plants regularly
Remove leaves and debris from pond
    frequently
Cut back foxglove spikes after flowering;
    may rebloom
For clearer water, drop submerged aquatic
    plants into water each spring

off the bricks, leave them for two hours, then scrub away any mortar stains with a wet cloth dipped in vinegar.

Cover the bricks with the plastic sheet for twenty-four hours to allow the mortar to dry slowly. Place the cherub on the edge of the brick. Fill the shell with water to the rim.

Plant the foxgloves and love-in-a-mist around the pond. They'll self-seed from year to year. Watch children around foxgloves; every part of the plant is very poisonous.

RAISED POND
WITH WOODEN SEAT

As summer winds down into fall, the fountain still runs, but herons have taken the goldfish, and duckweed dropped from the birds' feet is colonizing the water surface. Soon the pond will swell with rain, later with glassy ice and snow.

Usually in March the sun breaks through, and the pond seat is the first place to head for. Glittering ice shards crack and sink into the water. Clusters of ivy berries, black brooches on the snow during winter, roll along the pond bottom among fall's maple and beech leaves. It's just warm enough, with a slant of sunshine on the seat, to sit and dream about summer.

HOW TO DO IT 回回

This pond is composed of a black liner inside a rectangle of stacked four-by-six treated beams. The fountain is a simple plastic extension on a small pump that sits in the pond. Before you begin, check that the electrical cable on the pump will reach a GFI outlet nearby. If necessary, order a pump with a longer cable, or have a GFI outlet installed by an electrician.

Choose a flat area for the pond, on concrete or dirt or lawn. If necessary, clear weeds or remove turf, and rake the ground level.

Place the beams three deep in a rectangle. Stack them wider sides down so that the 4-inch edges make the pond sides (approximately 12 inches high). For the liner and seat to fit, the long sides of the pond must overlap the short sides (the pond interior measures 5 feet by approximately 6 feet).

Check that the pond corners are square; measure the distances between the diagonal corners, they should be the same. Using the level on top of the piece of two-by-four, check that the pond frame is perfectly level; when the pond is filled, the waterline will draw attention to even a slight slope.

On the long sides of the pond, drill holes 2½ inches from the corners for the bolts, three bolts per corner, one to join each pair of butting beams. Hammer the bolts into place.

Check the soil inside the frame; remove any stones or roots close to the surface. Lay the underlayment, or spread 1½ inches of damp compacted sand. (The liner can go directly onto concrete; just sweep the concrete clean first.)

Unroll the liner and drape it into the frame until there's a uniform 6-inch overlap on all sides. Smooth out the creases into the corners; tuck them into one large pleat behind the liner. Place the bricks on the pond edges to secure the overlap. Be careful that no sharp object punctures the liner.

Run 6 inches of water into the pond. The water will press the liner to the pond floor and sides. If the liner starts to strain, give it slack by moving the bricks.

Place the seat boards on the pond sides, removing the bricks, and tucking the liner neatly under the seat. The seat should overhang the water by a couple of inches all around, to hide the liner. Nail down the seat at the corners, 4 nails per corner.

Put a brick into the pond, and sit the pump on it. The pump needs to be off the bottom so that it doesn't become clogged with sediment. To protect the

Moderately inexpensive
Moderately easy
Location: Sun or light shade

Tools
Hoe, sharp-edged spade, and rake, to clear ground, if necessary
Measuring tape
Level
Straight piece of two-by-four, 6½ feet long, for checking level
Drill, to make bolt holes
Hammer
Pruning shears or knife, to remove roots, if necessary
Hose
Shovel, for spreading sand (optional)
Hand-held tamper, for compacting sand (optional)
Dustpan and small broom, if pond sits on concrete

Ingredients
Pond frame, treated four-by-six beams:
    for the sides, 6 beams 7 feet long
    for the ends, 6 beams 5 feet long
12 bolts, ½ inch in diameter, at least 7 inches long
Pond underlayment or old carpet, 5 by 6 feet; or 5 cubic feet of builder's sand
Pond liner, black, EPDM or butyl or PVC, 30 to 45 mil, 8 by 9 feet
12 bricks, to use as weights and pump support
Seat boards, treated two-by-twelve planks, ends mitered by supplier at 45-degree angle:
    for the sides, 2 planks 7½ feet long
    for the ends, 2 planks 6½ feet long
16 nails, 3 inches long
Submersible pump, 140 to 180 GPH, with flow adjuster and fountain extension
1 shrubby bamboo or vine

Maintenance
Refill pond regularly
Remove leaves and flowers from pond regularly
Keep pump intake clear
In severe winters, remove pump before water freezes
After rainy season, scrub wood to remove any moss

pump further, and reduce maintenance, see page 38. Attach the fountain extension to the pump outlet; it needs to clear the water surface, so raise the pump on another brick if necessary. Lay the electrical cable over the seat on the far side of the pond, and disguise it by planting a shrubby bamboo or vine there.

Fill the pond. Plug the electrical cable into the GFI outlet, and turn the fountain on. Adjust the water flow on the pump until you like the sound and height of the fountain.

LILY POND, FOUNTAIN JAR, AND GOLDFISH

Honeywort and forget-me-nots on the bank grew taller than expected and billowed out over the brick into the water, creating dappled places behind a screen of blue flowers where the fish can hide. Algae gave the new terra-cotta fountain a pretty patina, then developed into emerald ropes that the water bubbles slide onto and sail down.

The owners like to watch what nature will do. They'll leave the two lily pads flattened against the jar, so the fountain water flows over them and off the tips in a gleaming stream. But they may intervene to stop the carpet of fern from choking the crystal water channels that mirror the lilies as they open.

HOW TO DO IT 回回 This pond is a 5-by-12-foot rectangle made with a black liner. It's edged with loose, unmortared bricks and a planted bank. The pump for the bubbling jar sits in the pond; a metal pipe inserted through a hole in the base of the jar carries water to the surface and spills it out over the rim. The pond is heavily planted and contains goldfish. A bridge provides the only access to the water. Before you begin, check that the electrical cable on the pump will reach a GFI outlet nearby. If necessary, order a pump with a longer cable, or have a GFI outlet installed by an electrician. Ask a friend to help you drape the liner into the pond.

Choose a flat area for the pond. Clear any weeds, and rake the ground level. Outline the rectangle—5 by 12 feet—with twine and stakes, and excavate the area to a depth of 24 inches. As much as you can, leave the soil at the pond edges undisturbed and firm. Slope the sides a little toward the bottom, and work carefully, to keep the sides stable. Remove the excavated soil to another area of the garden; the ground surrounding the pond should be level or fall away a little, to prevent runoff into the pond.

Check that the pond edges are perfectly level. For the long edges, place the level atop the piece of two-by-four. When the pond is filled, the waterline will draw attention to even a slight slope. Remove any rocks, cut back protruding roots, and firm the bottom of the hole with the back of the spade or the tamper.

Lay the underlayment in the bottom of the pond. Unroll the liner, and drape it into the pond. At this point don't worry about how it fits, just tip it in until there's a uniform 1-foot overlap on all sides. Place bricks on the pond edges to secure the overlap. Be careful that no sharp object punctures the liner.

Place the hose in the pond and turn on the water, gently, until the water is 3 inches deep. The water will press the liner to the pond floor and sides. If the liner starts to strain, give it slack by moving the bricks. Smooth out the creases into the corners; tuck them into one large pleat behind the liner. Place bricks on the edges to secure the pleats.

Before you fill the pond with water, build and position the fountain. Work from inside the pond, and be careful not to disturb the banks behind the liner. If the jar has no drainage hole, drill one in the center of the base; make it ¾

Moderately expensive
Moderately difficult
Location: Sun

Tools
Rake
Twine and stakes, for marking out pond
Straight-edged spade, for digging
Wheelbarrow
Level
Straight piece of two-by-four, 12 feet long
Pruning shears or knife, to remove roots, if necessary
Hand-held tamper (optional)
Hose
Drill with ¾-inch masonry bit, if jar has no drainage hole
Spatula or knife, for applying caulking
Planting trowel

Ingredients
Pond underlayment:
    for pond bottom, 5 by 12 feet; or 2 inches of damp sand; or old carpet
    for pad under fountain, 2 square feet
Pond liner, black, EPDM or butyl or PVC, 30 to 45 mil, 11 by 18 feet
Bricks, old or new, approx. 160
Water jar, with or without drainage hole, approx. 20 inches tall and 12 inches across at rim, frost-proof if necessary
Submersible pump, 180 GPH, with flow adjuster
Plastic tubing, 4 feet long, flexible but thick-walled, diameter to fit pump outlet
Copper pipe, ½ inch in diameter, 1 inch longer than height of water jar
Silicone caulking
Straight piece of four-by-twelve, 8 feet long, for bridge
2 water lilies (*Nymphaea* 'Texas Dawn')
5 plastic pots, 12 inches in diameter, with or without drainage holes, for aquatic plants
Fertilizer pellets formulated for lilies
Gravel, 1 small bag
15 bunches of oxygenating plants, a mix of species
Water fern (*Azolla* spp.), 1 scoop
Bank plants, such as water forget-me-not (*Myosotis scorpioides*), iris, honeywort (*Cerinthe major*), coral bells (*Heuchera* spp.)
12 goldfish

inch wide. Decide on a place for the jar; take into account the position of the plank bridge.

Lay a piece of underlayment, then build a base for the jar by stacking bricks, in sets of four, almost to where the waterline will be when the pond is full.

Decide on a convenient place for the pump, close to the bridge for easy maintenance and within reach of the GFI outlet. Put two bricks on top of one another in the pond, and sit the pump on them. The pump needs to be off the bottom so that it doesn't become clogged with sediment. To protect the pump further, and reduce maintenance, see page 38.

Push one end of the plastic tubing over the outlet on the pump. Lay the electrical cable down into the pond and up over the rim in the direction of the GFI outlet. Note the positions of the flow adjuster on the pump and of the water intake.

Push the other end of the plastic tubing over the copper pipe so that it fits tightly. Insert the copper pipe through the hole in the bottom of the jar. Place the jar on top of the bricks, its base just below the waterline, and the copper pipe 1 inch below the rim of the jar.

Once the jar sits well on the bricks, use the level to check that it's perfectly even. If it's off kilter, the water will spill over only one part of the rim. Caulk around the pipe where it passes through the base of the jar; hold the pipe upright as you work. Recheck that the jar is perfectly level and the pipe vertical. Let the caulking dry for twenty-four hours (or follow instructions on the caulking tube).

Fill the pond with water, giving the liner slack as necessary. Check that the pond rim is still level. If necessary, fill any low points by pushing soil under the liner.

Fill the jar with water. Plug the electrical cable into the GFI outlet, and turn the fountain on. Adjust the water flow on the pump until you like the sound of the fountain.

Lay the bricks side by side around the rim to make an edging. Position them so that the ends overhang the water by 2 inches, to hide the liner. This is a decorative edge only. It is not safe to stand on.

Lay the plank bridge across the pond, the ends extending 18 inches onto

Maintenance
Refill pond regularly
Water bank plants regularly
Remove dead leaves and flowers from
    pond regularly
Feed lilies often, as recommended
Keep pump intake clear
In severe winters, remove pump before
    water freezes, and melt hole in ice to
    provide oxygen to fish

the banks. Its weight should rest squarely on the banks, away from the pond. If it rests on the pond edges, they may crumble. Remove bricks along the edge or move soil on the banks until the plank is stable.

Plant the lilies into two 12-inch pots, using soil excavated from the pond site. The crown (where the stems meet the tuber) must be just above the soil surface. Push lily fertilizer pellets into the soil, according to the instructions on the label. Place the gravel on the surface of the pots, to prevent the soil from floating into the water. Water each pot until it's completely water-logged, then lower it into the pond. (Keep the area around the pump free of plants.) Place bricks under the pot so that the lily crown sits between 8 and 12 inches below the water surface.

Plant the oxygenators. Fill three 12-inch pots with excavated soil, and push the stems into the soil, five bunches per pot. Cover the surface of the pots with gravel, water the pots thoroughly, and place them on the bottom of the pond.

Drop the water fern onto the surface of the pond.

Bury the edges of the pond liner, and plant the bank plants into the soil.

Wait at least two weeks before introducing the fish into the pond, so the chlorine has time to dissipate. Float the bag of fish on the water surface for twenty minutes before releasing the fish. To keep the water clear and the fish healthy, either don't feed them at all or feed them lightly—once a day with pelleted food and only as much as the fish eat in a few minutes; stop feeding in winter.

DRY WATERFALL AND POOL

Water seems to collect in this steep dry garden as it does in the Sierra Nevada, in basins and pools at the foot of granite cascades. Blue fescue grasses line the imagined watercourse, as if they had all seeded in the moist slope last spring. In the dry crevices, out of the reach of the wind, gray-white succulents absorb the radiated warmth from the rocks. At the pool, there's moisture year round, and therefore easy, rich green growth. The water surface is a colony of bright duckweed. When it is cleared or a breeze waves it apart, the shadows of the lily-of-the-Nile become glittery reflections.

HOW TO DO IT 回回

These rocks suggest a waterfall; there's no flowing water. The pool is made by hand, of concrete; the materials are mixed together and then sculpted while wet directly into an excavated basin. The waterfall requires a slope. In a wet climate, if rainwater runs down the slope and into the pool, divert it into a drainage pipe at the foot of the slope, or be prepared to clear debris out of the pool each spring. In very frosty climates, concrete is likely to crack when the water in the pool freezes; unless you're experienced in working with concrete, in cold climates make the pool with a liner, or sink a container into the ground. Only the blue fescues are frost hardy; substitute cold-tolerant plants where necessary. The rocks in the cascade are heavy; ask a friend to help you place them.

Build the waterfall: To transport the boulders onto the slope, use a number of different tools, as necessary. You might move them on a platform (a sheet of plywood, or carpet if the rocks have moss or algae that might get scratched) sitting atop three long poles that you can then use as rollers. Use a fourth pole to lever them on and off the platform. Or secure rope or chain around the rocks, with carpet pads to help prevent scuffs, and drag them; tie a pole into the rope to turn the rocks over. Once they're on the slope, a bar is useful to turn them into exactly the right place. Never try to lift heavy rocks; instead, raise them by rolling them up a plank set on an incline. Wear strong boots and gloves, and stand clear of the rocks as you're moving them.

Start at the foot of the slope. Secure the boulders by sinking them back and down into the bank. As you work, imagine water flowing between and over the boulders; create channels between rock faces if you can. Avoid stacking the boulders in too much of a line, one above the other. Be absolutely certain that each boulder is stable before you bring in the next one (perhaps secure the boulders with concrete where necessary). Work from the sides of the cascade, your feet and legs out of the way of falling rocks.

Build the pool: dig a hole 18 inches deep at the center, tapering to 5 inches deep at the edges, roughly elliptical in shape—approximately 2½ feet across and 4 feet long. The pool looks natural because of its irregular shape, so make the curves a little different on each side. Tamp the soil with the back of the spade or with the planting trowel until it is firm.

Put on the rubber gloves to keep the cement off your skin. In the bucket or wheelbarrow, thoroughly combine the dry materials for the concrete—1 part cement, 3 parts sand, and 1 part pea gravel. Measure the materials in level

Moderately inexpensive
Moderately difficult
Location: Sun or partial shade

Tools

Wheelbarrow and other implements for moving boulders, such as plywood platform or carpet, 4 long poles, rope, chain, bar, plank for incline (see text)
Measuring tape
Spade, for digging
Rubber gloves
Bucket or wheelbarrow, for mixing concrete
Shovel, for mixing concrete
Hose or watering can
Builder's trowel, triangular
Pliers for cutting chicken wire
Plastic sheet or wet cloths, if weather turns wet or hot
Paintbrush, 4 inches wide
Planting trowel

Ingredients

Boulders, local, 2 feet across, interesting surfaces, 1 per 1 foot of slope
Concrete, approx. 10 cubic feet, composed of
    1 part cement (2 cubic feet)
    3 parts river or stucco sand (6 cubic feet)
    1 part pea gravel (2 cubic feet)
Chicken wire, 5 by 7 feet
Acrylic resin sealer
Blue fescues (*Festuca ovina* 'Glauca'), 2 per 1 foot of slope
Hen and chicks (*Echeveria elegans*), 1 per 1 foot of slope
2 lily-of-the-Nile (*Agapanthus orientalis*)
Duckweed (*Lemna* spp.), 1 scoop
Small fish or mosquito larvae control that contains *B. t. israelensis*

Maintenance

Water plants regularly until established, then less frequently
Replace mosquito control (optional) as necessary
Empty and scrub pool occasionally if you wish

shovelfuls. Once the mix is uniform, add water gradually, turning and mixing as you go until it's "a little wetter than sand for sand castles," says the designer, Harland Hand. Wet is better than dry (too dry and it won't set properly). If the mix becomes too wet, add more cement and sand.

Kneeling on the pond edge, use the builder's trowel to pack the concrete into the hole to a uniform thickness of 2 inches. Proceed section by section around the hole so that you can check the thickness of the concrete against the soil. Pack the concrete firmly, to push out any air bubbles, which could cause a leak. When this first layer of concrete is in place, line the hole with the chicken wire, and press it against the bottom and sides. The chicken wire will act as reinforcing between the layers of concrete.

Apply the second layer of concrete, another 2 inches in the same fashion. Trim the chicken wire to within 2 inches of the rim, roll up the edge of the wire, and pack concrete around it, to form a thick lip.

Tamp and smooth the surfaces with the trowel, to remove air pockets. Sculpt the sides into pleasing contours; when the water is clear, you'll see inside. Sprinkle three handfuls of dry cement around the basin and lip, and trowel it to an even, glassy shine. Wash the concrete off the tools before it dries.

Wait two weeks for the concrete to cure. Cover the pool with the plastic sheet if it starts to rain. Cover it with the wet cloths if the weather turns hot and dry.

Apply two coats of the acrylic resin with the brush, to waterproof the pool and make it resistant to corrosion. When the resin is dry, fill the pool with water.

Plant the fescues at the edges of the waterfall and the hen and chicks in the rock crevices. Plant one lily-of-the-Nile at each end of the pool. Drop the duckweed onto the water surface. For mystery, do as Harland does: let algae form and debris drift into the water, to darken it.

To keep mosquitoes from breeding in the pool, introduce small fish or sprinkle a biological control into the water.

SPRINGS AND DITCHES

On mountain slopes, if water can't drain fast enough into the soil, it flows along the surface, slipping over cliffs and seeping from banks on its way downhill. In those places, the air is moist and cool from the splash, rainbows appear at certain times of day, and droplets shine on gold marsh marigolds growing in soggy moss. The water carries along mountain leaves and twigs that have fallen into the flow.

On flat land, water that can't drain fills ditches. There it stays, a swirling pale chocolate brown for a while, only the whitest clouds and blackest branches reflected in it. Gradually the silt settles over the feet of rushes or irises. Water striders skate in the clear water channels between the stems; glittering stretches mirror the iris blooms.

A steep garden, or a flat garden that won't drain, is traditionally considered pitiful luck for the gardener. In fact, each offers a beautiful opportunity for a spring or ditch. The three recipes in this chapter originate in gardens with challenging terrains. Roger Raiche's Sulfur Springs sits in a cliff that looms over the back of his house. It's an adventure climbing the small trail to find the source of the echoing water splash; it takes you up above the roofline of the house to views of the bay.

Ron Lutsko built his rill not only to prevent drainpipe water from flooding back under the house but also to savor the rare rainwater for as long as possible, to see and hear it swish through turns and steps, and to have it water the only damp piece of ground in his droughty hillside garden.

Sarah Hammond dug her ditch to drain the flood that appeared in her garden one winter when a nearby road was paved and the culvert set too high. The simple bridges over the ditch were makeshift necessities that became garden accents once the banks were planted. People love to cross over a water boundary, knowing they must later cross back — the imagination teases the mind with visions of a flood rising over the plank.

If you have a damp spot, you have a bog garden. Mark the spot loudly with plants that people associate with water — reeds, irises, native wetland plants. Spread the plants as far afield as the moisture reaches, or cheat and water the outlying area to make the bog seem larger. But keep the wettest part somewhat free of plants, so that you see the whirligigs and the reflections of the reeds against the sky. Place a plank or stepping-stones across the wettest part, for the thrill of standing an inch above bog water and waist high in water irises.

A dry bank, not a wet bank, is the easiest place to build a spring, because it's generally more stable. It's fun to divert rainwater, but double-check that none will drain toward building foundations or property lines.

SULFUR SPRINGS

Roger Raiche's Sulfur Springs is a shrine to two favorite things: abandoned mines and roadside springs. Coils of rusty wire and broken pieces of concrete, stained with iron sulfate to a burnt ruin color, are scattered on the hillside. Rusty containers, rebar, and a fire grill lie on the side of the path. Like a flooded pit in an old mine, the pond contains rusted tools and fallen rocks and is silted with rust flakes and nails.

Into this ruin flows water fresh as rainfall. It gurgles out of a pipe, swills about in a basin in the sunshine, then drops in a glistening splash to the pond. Spray droplets nourish the rosettes of thrifty pink-gray succulents reproducing behind the wire, and new green leaves are beginning to cover the rust.

HOW TO DO IT 🔳🔳

This spring is fed by a pump hidden under bricks in the pond. A flexible pipe takes water 3 feet up the bank, retained with a low wall, to the spring. Apart from the pump, the components and materials are all found objects, salvaged from friends and industrial recycling centers. This recipe is a construction adventure; the basics are described, but the choice of materials is purposefully left loose, for experimentation and scavenger's luck. Before you buy the pump, check that the electrical cable will reach a GFI outlet nearby. If necessary, order a pump with a longer cable, or have a GFI outlet installed by an electrician.

Choose a site for the spring. For a natural look, place it against a hillside or bank; a wall might do if you plant around and above it, to give a sense of natural steepness. Try to allow for access to the water; in Roger's garden, a path crosses the pond on stepping-stones, so the spring and basin are within arm's reach.

Consider the pitch of the slope, how rainwater drains off it. Grade the bank if necessary to ensure that rain will drain across the slope. You don't want water to flow off the bank into the pond or to accumulate in the soil behind the retaining wall. If your bank is loose or waterlogged after storms, consult a contractor about a simple drainage system before you begin.

Put on old clothes, gloves, and boots before you open the iron sulfate; the powder stains everything. Decide on the objects to stain—the stones, basin, clay pipe, stepping-stones, anything you want to make part of the ruin theme. With a little water, mix a thick paste in the bucket, and sponge it heavily onto the objects (less heavily for a lighter stain). As you finish sponging each object, mist it with a very fine spray of water from the hose. Try to keep the powder and paste off plants, because iron sulfate will damage foliage and can kill a plant if it touches the crown. Some damage is almost inevitable if you are staining objects settled into a planted bank, so remove any precious plants before you start.

For a strong deep stain, the objects need to dry slowly. Apply the stain late in the evening or on a cool overcast day. If the day is warm, cover the objects with the tarp, and occasionally mist underneath it. The stain dries well in four or five hours. Repeat the staining if the color is lighter than you wanted.

Moderately inexpensive
Moderately difficult
Location: Sun or partial shade

Tools

Old bucket, for mixing stain
Sponge
Hose, with misting nozzle
Tarp, to cover stained objects, if necessary
Twine and stakes
Straight-edged spade
Pruning shears or knife, to remove roots, if necessary
Level
Planting trowel

Ingredients

Iron sulfate (sold as soil acidifier in nurseries), 5 to 10 pounds
Bricks and stones, flat-sided, for retaining wall, including 2 large cornerstones and several long stretcher stones
Bricks for pond edge, pond decoration, pump support, pot supports (optional), and stepping-stone supports
Basin, any material, shape, and size
Assortment of rusty metal and clay pipes, for spring, various diameters so that one fits inside another; smallest pipe large enough to hold plastic tubing from pump
Concrete block, to contain and support pipes at springhead
Plastic tubing, flexible but thick-walled, to run from pump to top of spring, diameter to fit pump outlet
Pond container, rigid black tray or tank at least 8 inches deep
Submersible pump, 320 to 400 GPH, with flow adjuster
Rocks, coiled wire, to decorate bank
Plants for bank, including vining ground covers such as a small bramble or thimbleberry (*Rubus* spp.) and ivy (*Hedera* spp.), and otherworldly plants, such as pink succulents (*Aeonium* spp. or *Echeveria* spp.) and lime-purple geranium (*Pelargonium* spp.)
Plants in pots, to hide pond corners (optional)
Rusty tools and nails, for pond decoration
2 stepping-stones, large broken pieces of concrete or paving stone

Wash the finished objects thoroughly, to remove any residue that might harm plants. Wait a week before planting.

Retain the slope with a low wall of brick and stones. Put on sturdy boots and gloves. Place the largest stones first, at the corners. Work toward the center, laying the stones flattest side down, canting them into the bank for stability, and filling between them with bricks and small stones. Place occasional long "stretcher" stones across the smaller stones, for stability. Be sure the wall is stable.

Clear a ledge for the basin at the top of the wall. Settle the basin so that the bank, not the wall, takes its weight. If the basin is heavy and the bank loose, excavate behind the wall, and build a firm base of stones for it. Consider how water will spill from the basin when it's full. If it has a natural lip, center the lip over the pond. If the rim is level, you'll need to tilt the basin toward the pond a little so that the water spills only on that side and not into the bank.

Clear a place in the bank behind the basin for the spring. Assemble your Russian doll arrangement of pipes inside the concrete block. The smallest rusty pipe protrudes from the rest, over the basin, and the plastic tubing is hidden inside it. Place the concrete block on the bank. Its weight must rest squarely on the bank, not the edge of the basin.

Clear a level area up against the wall for the pond. Mark out the pond outline with the twine and stakes. Excavate to the depth of the pond container. Remove any rocks or roots protruding from the soil. Check that the pond edges are level. When the pond is filled, the waterline will draw attention to even a slight slope. Place the pond container into the excavation. Check that it's level.

Place a brick in the corner of the pond nearest the GFI outlet, and sit the pump on it. The pump needs to be off the bottom so that it doesn't become clogged with sediment. To protect the pump further, and reduce maintenance, see page 38.

Push the end of the plastic tubing from the spring over the outlet on the pump. Lay the electrical cable down into the pond and up over the rim in the direction of the GFI outlet.

Fill the pond and basin with water. Plug the electrical cable into the GFI

Maintenance
Refill pond regularly
Water plants regularly
Keep pump intake clear
In severe winters, remove pump
    before water freezes

outlet, and turn on the pump. Adjust the water flow on the pump until you like the sound of the waterfall. Break the splash by placing bricks in the pond if you like. Check that the water is spilling well from the spring; tilt the pipe toward the pond if necessary to stop water from running back into the bank.

Once the water is flowing as you like it, finish the details: Scatter rocks and coils of wire on the bank, bury the plastic tubing or hide it behind rocks, and plant the creeping plants around the spring. Place bricks around the edges of the pond, to hide the pond container; place bricks over the pump to hide it; place the container plants on piles of brick to hide the pond corners (optional); and drop the tools and nails into the water.

Place the stepping-stones carefully. One end of each stone must rest on the path, the other on a sturdy pile of bricks in the pond. For safety, make sure the weight of the stone is not pivoted on the pond edge.

LADY FERN GORGE, BRICK RILL

After months of drought, rain starts to patter on the porch roof. Instead of disappearing silently underground, unseen, the water trickles out from the drainpipe in a waterfall, gurgles under lady ferns through the brick-lined gorge, and emerges as a gleaming ribbon in the rill.

The water noises echo around the porch during the shower. Rain drips from the ferns and sedges, soaks the brick, makes mud on the banks. Red maple leaves swim in the ½-inch flood. A few showers more and the ferns will start to grow fiddleheads; moss will appear on the bricks. When the drought returns, the rill is a reassurance that it will rain again one day.

HOW TO DO IT 🔲🔲 This water feature carries rainwater from a drainpipe down a slope away from the house. The design requires such a slope. The water runs through a flexible drainpipe to a clay pipe set in the bank; from there it falls into a rill lined with unmortared bricks. The water seeps between the bricks, irrigating the ferns, the flow diminishing as it moves down the slope. The rill ends at a path; the water drips into a pipe that runs under the path, and then spills freely down over the garden.

Before you begin, assess where your drainage water will flow out. On a small property, to keep the water flow from causing problems for your neighbors, you may need to collect the water at the end of the rill into a more sophisticated drainage system designed by a landscape architect.

Decide on a route for the water. Start the rill 1 or 2 yards from the house, to keep the water away from the house foundation. Perhaps run it alongside a path or porch, where the water will be seen and heard. Zigzag the route, to lengthen it and create corners for the water to run around. Mark out the edges of the rill with the twine and stakes. Make it 12 inches wide.

Dig a trench from the base of the house drainpipe to the top of the waterfall; make it large enough to accommodate the flexible drainpipe. Lay the drainpipe in the trench. Position the waterfall pipe at the head of the falls. Push the end of the flexible drainpipe at least 4 inches inside the waterfall pipe.

Dig the rill trench. The depth of the trench will vary according to your slope and route. Start out with a deep trench at the waterfall, so the water from the pipe will plunge into a gorge, splashing and echoing against the sides. Slope the trench bottom gradually downhill, so that the water chuckles along—too steep and the water will be gone in a flash. Create an occasional step; the water will make a pretty sound as it skips over the drop.

Line the rill with bricks. In the center of the trench, directly below the waterfall pipe, place the bricks lengthwise, wide sides down, one in front of the other, without gaps, to make the watercourse. To make the rill walls, stack bricks on the sides of the watercourse. In the gorge, for stability, lay them lengthwise, wide sides down, without gaps. The watercourse should be about 4 inches wide, and the walls 1 or 2 inches above the soil surface, so that soil doesn't wash into the rill. Firm the soil on the bank against the outside of the brick walls.

Inexpensive
Moderately easy
Location: Sun or partial shade

Tools
Twine and stakes
Measuring tape
Straight-edged spade, for digging
Hose
Planting trowel

Ingredients
Flexible drainpipe:
    1 piece to fit over house drainpipe
      and reach into waterfall pipe
    1 piece to reach from rill drain to
      lower in the garden (see text)
Clay drainpipe for waterfall, 4 inches in
    diameter, 12 inches long
Bricks, approx. 15 per 1 yard of rill on
    shallow stretches, 60 per 1 yard
    through gorge, plus some to place
    across rill to contain splashing, if
    necessary
Clamp, to connect flexible drainpipe to
    house drainpipe
Lady ferns (*Athyrium filix-femina*, crested
    form), 1 per 2 feet of upper rill edge
1 umbrella plant (*Darmera peltata*)
3 irises (*Iris ensata*), to make 1 clump at
    waterfall
Sedges (*Carex nudata*), 2 per 1 yard of
    lower rill edge
1 maple (*Acer palmatum* 'Dissectum
    Atropurpureum')

Maintenance
Water plants regularly
Clean debris from rill during wet season

As the walls get shorter, you can lay the wall bricks on their narrow edges if you like. Out of the gorge, the rill has just one wall brick on either side, narrow side down, as shown in the photograph.

At the bottom of the rill, make a drain 12 inches square and 12 inches deep. From the drain, dig a 12-inch-deep trench under a path or down the slope, to surface where the water will not erode the soil or cause drainage problems. Lay flexible drainpipe in the trench. Bend the pipe into the center of the drain, and line the floor and walls with bricks.

To try out the rill, place the hose into the flexible drainpipe at the top of the slope, and turn on the water. Close any large gaps between bricks, but allow some water to seep between them. In the upper reaches of the rill, if necessary, place bricks across the rill to stop water from splashing up out of it onto the banks.

Connect the flexible drainpipe to the house drainpipe with the clamp. Cover the flexible drainpipe with soil. Plant the lady ferns, umbrella plant, and irises on the banks at the top end of the rill, the sedges on the lower banks. Plant the maple tree 3 feet above or to one side of the waterfall.

DRAINAGE DITCH WITH ROSES

The path turns away from the house, winds around a bush germander and arrives suddenly at a bridge. Crossing over, you find a startling new view: a long slit through the earth, draped with rosemary and thyme, runs under David Austin and hybrid musk roses right across the garden.

In summer, people stop on the bridges because of the fragrance, the cool-looking shadows under the bridges, and the simple pleasure of being suspended between banks. In January, when rainfall and runoff have filled the ditch, inch by inch, every trip out into this part of the garden means crossing a mirror shiny with reflections of gray bush germander spikes, dark cypress trees, and the cold pearly blue sky.

HOW TO DO IT 🔁🔁 This ditch carries runoff during the wet season to a network of ditches linked to the county-built ditch. It's 3 feet wide and about 2½ feet deep. The bridges simply rest on the banks, without permanent foundations. Before you begin, assess where your drainage water will flow out. On a small property, to keep the water flow from causing problems for your neighbors, you may need a more sophisticated drainage system designed by a landscape architect.

Mark out the boundary of the ditch with the twine and stakes. Make it 3 feet wide.

Dig the ditch, shoveling the soil up onto the banks, to raise the level of the planting beds so the soil will drain even more freely. Slope the sides of the ditch if you need to, so that they are stable.

Spread the excavated soil evenly over the surrounding garden. On top of it, spread a 4-inch layer of manure or compost. Dig or rototill the garden to a depth of 8 inches. The soil is now sufficiently improved for planting. Firm the banks of the ditch if you've disturbed them while working the ground.

Build the bridges: For each bridge, place two four by four runners across the ditch, 3 feet apart, ends protruding evenly onto the banks. Settle the runners until they are well supported and the tops are 1½ inches below soil level. Check that the runners are level.

Lay four plank two-by-twelves across the runners, overhanging the runners 6 inches on each side. Set them square, and align the crack between the middle two planks exactly on the center of the ditch. Nail the planks to the runners, using 2 nails at each end of each plank. Firm the soil at the ends of the bridge.

Plant the Mexican daisies at the bridge corners. Plant the thyme 1 foot apart and the rosemaries 4 feet apart along the banks. Place the bush germanders and roses, 4 feet apart, to block views of the ditch as the paths approach it. Find places for the evening primroses close to the bridges; in summer, their scent will mingle with that of the roses.

Inexpensive
Easy
Location: Sun

Tools
Twine and stakes
Measuring tape
Straight-edged spade, for digging
Shovel, for spreading soil and manure
Rotary cultivator (optional)
Level
Hammer
Planting trowel

Ingredients
Manure or compost, 3 cubic feet per
    1 square yard of planting area
Redwood, heartwood cedar, or treated
    wood; for each bridge:
    2 four-by-fours, 6 feet long, for bridge
        runners
    4 two-by-twelves, 4 feet long, for top
        of bridge
16 nails for each bridge
Mexican daisies (*Erigeron karvinskianus*),
    1 for each corner of each bridge
Thyme (*Thymus serpyllum* or *T. praecox
    arcticus*), 9 per 1 square yard, and
    rosemaries (*Rosmarinus officinalis* 'Ken
    Taylor'), 1 per 1 square yard, to cover
    banks
Bush germanders (*Teucrium fruticans*) and
    roses (*Rosa* 'Penelope' and 'Graham
    Thomas'), as needed to block views
    of ditch
Evening primroses (*Oenothera berlandieri*
    'Siskiyou'), 3 at each bridge

Maintenance
Water plants regularly until established,
    then less frequently
In late fall, prune and trim all plants,
    especially evening primrose

WATERY EFFECTS

A watery effect can be conjured simply. Water is suggested in an empty watering can. If it's a metal one, the sight of it virtually contains the sound of water from the faucet drumming against the bottom and singing over the rim. If it's an old one, there must be mud in the handle somewhere from years of work in the vegetable garden. A pair of large gray metal watering cans sitting under a fresh green potted maple on a hot porch cools the air and makes a lovely welcome.

The imagination is triggered by detail. A gazing ball evokes water not just because of its reflective qualities but also because the surface is smooth and cool and the reflections wavy and distorted. Delaney, Cochran, and Castillo's metaphorical canal is blue, but it's also large in the landscape, and the flowers ruffle in the wind just like water.

In a dry creek bed, smooth river-washed pebbles are clues to water, as are the swings in the banks, the erosion on the outsides of the curves, the silt and leaves among the pebbles. Grasses and other airy plants bounce light about, and shadows of them flicker over the river boulders, like water moving. The stones should be big enough to hop from one to the next, at least in one's mind. A boulder that's been washed away from the bank would be the place to stretch out and listen to the water running by.

As you build, think water—its colors, shine, and shadows, its movement over the ground, the traces it leaves behind. Aim to capture some of its qualities beautifully, but don't try to build a literal picture, which may come too close to an embarrassing deception. The imagination needs space to play.

In dry zen gardens, a very few elements, immaculately well chosen and contrivingly placed, can release the imagination into journeys of peace and meditation. Water flows in a huge sea around islands of rock, the movement recorded in swirls on a flat bright plane. The eye follows the lines into the coves and round the promontories and back out into the open sea. Between two islands, a tight channel holds a fjord overshadowed by cliffs; away from the mountains, the water laps against miles and miles of sand.

A garden that engages the imagination is fun to make and enchanting to experience. It draws you in as a participant in its spirit. It evokes feelings of play, gives the everyday literal mind a much-needed rest.

SEA LAVENDER SWALE

The swale swings in an abstract, or amoeboid, curve through a clearing on a hillside. Everything around the swale moves in symphony: bands of lawn swirl along the banks, ground covers loop alongside them. In the swale, water-washed rocks flow in arcs around the pebble watercourse. The interlocking shapes ride together voluptuously over the surface of the land.

There's movement also in the planting. The wind that whistles in the black-green forest is a whisper down here by the sun-soaked pale purple and yellow swale. It swishes the sea lavender bushes around the river rocks, creating watery shadows; it nudges the pool of wachendorfia, and it ebbs away through the shivering yellow-green bamboo.

HOW TO DO IT 🔲🔲 This swale is large—15 feet wide at the source and 40 feet long. It's placed as if it would catch water, but no water actually flows here. A brook is suggested by the boulders, river rocks, and pebbles and by the swale shape and the positioning of the plants. The boulders are very large; have two or three people help you drag, roll, and tip them into position, or ask the supplier whether the delivery team can install them. In cold climates, use hardier plants, such as umbrella plant *(Darmera peltata),* royal ferns *(Osmunda regalis),* and cupid's dart *(Catananche caerulea).*

Choose a site for the swale. To make it look natural, place it in a low-lying part of the garden or tipping gently across a sloping lawn.

Mark out the perimeter with the twine and stakes. Create a generous bulge (about 15 feet wide) at the top of the swale, nearest the "water source"; then swing the banks through a wide curve, bringing them closer gradually; next swing them in a smaller curve around the wachendorfia to disappear into a screen of trees or shrubs. If there's a sweep in the lines of existing trees or lawns, have the banks of the swale swing with those lines; it will exaggerate the sense of movement beautifully.

Mark out the pebble watercourse within the swale, with more twine and stakes. Start it fairly high up the slope in the bulge area and run it a little higher than centered between the banks until it turns the first curve; from there let it slip along the lower bank, as if gravity had pulled it downhill. Make the watercourse about 5 feet wide at the bulge, 4 feet wide where it disappears beside the bamboo.

Map out the rest of the swale in your mind. Most of the sea lavenders fill the lower part of the bulge and run to the first curve, like a marsh irrigated by the swale water seeping sideways down the slope. The low slab sits at the tip of the sea lavender marsh, on the edge of the bulge; the three broad boulders sit on the bank on the upper side of the watercourse. The river rocks trace an arc from the upper bank, around the bulge, and into the marsh. The wachendorfia and two euphorbias sit

Moderately expensive
Moderately difficult
Location: Sun

Tools
Twine and stakes, 2 sets
Measuring tape
Straight-edged spade, for digging out bank
Shovel, for spreading soil and pebbles
Wheelbarrow
Tools for moving boulders, such as plywood platform or carpet, 4 long poles, chain, rope, bar, plank for incline (see text)
Planting trowel
Hose or watering can

Ingredients
3 large broad boulders, river-washed, with very round surfaces, big enough for ⅓ to be buried, 1 flat enough for Buddha (optional)
1 large slab boulder, river-washed, with very round surfaces, big enough for ⅓ to be buried
Landscape cloth, to cover watercourse and river rock arc
Pebbles, river-washed, approx. 2 to 3 inches in diameter, 1½ wheelbarrow-fuls per 1 yard of watercourse
45 sea lavenders *(Limonium perezii)*
1 wachendorfia
5 euphorbias *(Euphorbia characias wulfenii)*
3 sedges *(Carex spp.)*
River rocks, river-washed, approx. 8 to 12 inches in diameter, 1 wheelbarrowful per 1 yard of arc
Stone Buddha (optional)

Maintenance
Water plants regularly until they are established, then less frequently
Cut euphorbia flower stalks to base when stalks yellow

at the end of the swale, forming a big clump around which the watercourse turns and disappears; the sedges dot the banks there. A few sea lavenders and euphorbias decorate the upper bank; the Buddha statue (optional) sits among them.

Before you bring in the rocks or plants, grade the swale. The downslope perimeter needs a defined bank; dig an 8-inch-deep trench along that side so that even with the rocks in the swale the water would not spill over the bank. Move the excavated soil across the watercourse onto the upslope bank. Check the pitch of the watercourse. It needs to slope gradually down to the bamboo and be fairly flat across its width.

Dig the holes for the boulders. Make them one-third of the boulder height. The deeper the boulders sit in the ground, the more they'll look like they've always been there.

Move each boulder into position using a number of different tools, as necessary. You might move it on a platform (a sheet of plywood, or carpet if the boulder has moss or algae that might get scratched) sitting atop three long poles that you can then use as rollers. Use a fourth pole to lever it on and off the platform. Or secure rope or chain around the boulder, with carpet pads to help prevent scuffs, and drag it; tie a pole into the rope to turn the boulder over. Once it's in the hole, a bar is useful to turn it into exactly the right place. Never try to lift the boulder; instead, raise it by rolling it up a plank set on an incline. Wear strong boots and gloves, and stand clear of the boulder as you're moving it.

Line the watercourse and the area for the arc of river rocks with the landscape cloth, to prevent weeds from growing up from the soil. Spread the pebbles in the watercourse. Plant the plants. Spread the river rocks around them in an arc. Cover any patches of landscape cloth with pebbles. Settle the Buddha (optional) on the flattest of the boulders.

STREAM OF PINK FLOWERS, PINK PEBBLES

The streambed is the first place children head for in this garden. They run off the pink flagstone patio into the meadow and up between the thick flowers on the banks as if crossing a forbidden boundary into water. The pink and mauve boulders are large enough for a child to hop on and off; they come from creeks in Idaho and Montana. The pockets of shade under them might harbor mud or water, somewhere for a frog or a water flea to hide.

While the children sort through the heart-shaped stones that garden designer Keeyla Meadows has collected over the years from beaches and arroyos, damselflies may alight in the stream. They emerge from the fountain basins in the garden, leave their filigreed larval cases on reeds, and come to the stream stones to bask in the sun.

HOW TO DO IT 回回

The stones and banks suggest a stream; no water flows here. The small slope is created by bringing in topsoil and compost.

Decide on a place for the stream source. A naturally high area in the garden is ideal. If your garden is flat, look for a place partially enclosed, such as an area in front of trees or tall shrubs; the plants will accentuate the height of the mound and hide the flat ground behind it.

Mark out the route of the stream with the stakes. Make the streambed about 20 inches wide, wider on the corners, where water would swing out and erode the bank. Take the stream through several turns, and let it spread out at the base into a flat area, or meadow.

Build the mound at the top of the stream. Make it about 20 inches high, and slope it gradually down toward the meadow. Firm the soil as you build, with your feet or the back of the shovel or the tamper.

Excavate the stream, starting at the meadow. Make a trench 4 inches deep. The bottom of the streambed should rise slightly all the way up to the source, so water would flow down it. But, for interest, make the upper section steeper; the streambed looks particularly pretty flowing between steep banks, as if water had carved a channel through the hillside. Shovel the soil from the excavation onto the banks.

Spread the compost 4 inches thick on the banks. Dig it in with the spade to a depth of at least 6 inches. Firm the banks. They are now ready for planting.

Place the biggest boulders toward the top of the stream and at the stream edges, but don't ring the edges with them or the stream will look unnatural. Scatter the pebbles down the streambed. Let some spill out into an alluvial fan at the meadow.

Place the urn at the top of the mound. Set it off to one side of the sight line up the middle of the stream. Fill the urn with potting soil. Plant the water-loving plants in the urn. Water them well. As they grow they'll spill over the sides; keep them well watered and fertilized so they always look abundant and moist.

Plant the banks. Place the forget-me-nots and baby blue eyes on the bank edges; they'll grow thickly into the stream. Plant the bulbs in pools under the bank. Plant the shrubs on the upper section of the stream, to lend more height to the slope.

Inexpensive
Easy
Location: Sun or light shade

Tools

Bamboo stakes, for marking out stream
Measuring tape
Shovel, for building mound and spreading compost
Hand-held tamper (optional)
Straight-edged spade, for digging trench
Planting trowel
Hose or watering can

Ingredients

Topsoil for mound and slope, if garden is flat, approx. 2 cubic yards
Compost, for improving soil on banks, 3 cubic feet per 1 square yard
Boulders, river-washed, Pamy or similarly colorful rock, ½ to 1 wheelbarrowful per 2 yards of stream
Pebbles, river-washed, range of sizes, Pamy or similarly colorful pebbles, approx. ½ to 1 wheelbarrowful per 2 yards of stream
Urn, tall, to lend height to water source
Potting soil, 1 bag
Plants for urn, such as 2 yellow marguerites (Chrysanthemum frutescens) and 6 pink and red tulips
Plant fertilizer
Plants for banks, such as blue and pink forget-me-nots (Myosotis spp.), baby blue eyes (Nemophila menziesii), clumps of 6 jonquil narcissus or muscari bulbs
Shrubs, such as pink sunrose (Helianthemum nummularium) and pink breath of heaven (Coleonema pulchrum)

Maintenance

Water plants regularly

METAPHORICAL FRENCH CANAL

Landscape architects Delaney, Cochran, and Castillo asked clients Barbara and Elliott Wolfe what they loved. French canals, they said. So they have one. They cross over it several times a day from the street to the front door, the blue lines running off to the far ends of the garden, narrowing in the distance.

In spring, blue blossoms appear in pools across the surface. Within weeks, the canal is solid blue, the light coming down through the magnolias, dappling and speckling the surface. In a summer shower, real puddles collect on the rolled paths, and get in the way of sparkling silver boules, just like a summer scene in the Jardin du Luxembourg in Paris. The wind ripples the flowers into a shimmer of pale blue and waves them over the canal sides.

HOW TO DO IT 回回

The canal is planted with low-growing blue Dalmatian bellflowers, which bloom from spring through summer and often again in fall. It is divided into two sections; a path between them provides the sensation of crossing the water. The canal sides are made of two blue painted boards.

Calculate the quantity of two-by-fours you'll need for each section of the canal as follows: First check the thickness of the wood; if it's treated wood, it's likely to be 1½ inches thick rather than 2 inches. For the long sides of each canal section, add twice the thickness of the wood to the canal length, and multiply by four (two boards on each side). For example, if the canal is 90 feet long, and the wood 1½ inches thick, you'll need 372 feet (90 + 1½ + 1½ = 93 x 4 = 372) for the sides. At each end of a canal section, you'll need one short piece the width of the canal, and one long piece the width of the canal plus four times the thickness of the wood (the inner end piece sits between the canal sides, the outer end piece overlaps the canal sides). For example, if the width of the canal is 5 feet, you'll need one 5-foot piece and one 5½-foot piece, if the wood is 1½ inches thick. Calculate the wood needed for each end of each canal section separately to allow for the tapering (described later). Perhaps buy the end pieces cut to size, and have the side pieces delivered in the longest stretches available.

Choose a flat site for the canal. Mark out the perimeter of the two sections of the canal with the twine and stakes; as you allow space for a path between the sections, bear in mind that the wood edges will protrude about 3 inches all around the canal perimeter.

Make the canal 5 feet wide at one end and taper it, to exaggerate the length, about 2 inches in every 7 feet. The Wolfes' canal is 90 feet long; it tapers from 5 feet to 3 feet. Place the wide end at the main viewing point so that the canal narrows and slims into the distance; from the narrow end the canal will look short and squat.

Paint the two-by-fours for the canal edges.

Prepare the soil for planting inside the canal perimeter. Spread 2 inches of compost over the surface and dig it in to a depth of at least 6 inches. Use a rotary cultivator if you like. Rake the ground level.

Dig a trench 3 inches deep and 3 inches wide around the canal (on the

Inexpensive
Moderately easy
Location: Sun or light shade

Tools
Twine and stakes
Measuring tape
Paintbrush
Shovel, for spreading compost
Straight-edged spade, for digging, or rotary cultivator
Rake
Wheelbarrow
Hammer
Saw
Planting trowel
Hose or watering can

Ingredients
Redwood, heartwood cedar, or treated two-by-fours for canal edges (see text for calculating amount)
Blue paint
Compost, 1½ cubic feet per 1 square yard of canal
Nails, 2½ inches long, 1 box
Stake one-by-twos, 9 inches long, for joints between boards on long sides of canal
Dalmatian bellflowers (*Campanula portenschlagiana*, or *C. muralis*), 2 per square foot

Maintenance
Water plants regularly
Sweep or hose dust off canal edges occasionally

outside of the twine) for the painted boards. Make the sides of the trench vertical, and the outside edge neat and level with the surrounding ground.

Lay the outside boards into the trench. Place them narrow side down, against the outside of the trench, the tops protruding about 1 inch above the surrounding ground. Start at a corner, laying the board that fits right across the end of the canal, the full width of the trench. Lay the board at the other end of the canal, again the full width of the trench; then lay the boards along the canal sides, between the end boards. Nail the corners together. Where pieces meet on the long sides, hammer a stake into the ground on the outside of the trench, and nail the boards to the stake, below ground level. Saw off the tops of the stakes. Firm the soil against the outsides of the boards.

Lay the inside boards. They look nice 1 inch higher than the outside ones, so with a trowel scoop 1 inch of soil from the canal into the trench, firm it with the back of the trowel, and lay the inside boards on top of it, up against the outside boards. This time, the end boards fit between the side boards. Nail the corners together. Where side pieces meet, nail them to stakes hammered into the ground on the canal side of the boards.

Plant the bellflowers in the canal, 9 inches apart.

GAZING BALL IN THE SHADE

A gazing ball pulls the small rectangle of sky above the apartment building down into the shady courtyard by the back cottage, stretching the light, fish-eyed, over the top of the ball. If a Boeing 747 or pelican flew over, it would appear in the garden; wisps of ocean fog swirl over sometimes, and once in a while rain clouds block the sun.

The lower part of the ball is swaddled in garden: baby's tears between warm pink brick; giant ferns, the ribs covered with brown fuzz; the steps of the cottage, lined with pink busy-lizzies; the cherry red garden gate and white metal chairs. Every bright blossom that grows down here in the shade is doubled in the ball.

People come and go across its surface, vivid elongated figures surrounded by paradise in the sunlight, eerie black shapes in the moonlight.

HOW TO DO IT 🔁🔁

This gazing ball rests on a pedestal anchored with a cluster of aeoniums. The ball is made of mirrored glass; it has a short stem, which rests inside the top of the pedestal.

Find a place for the gazing ball. Because it reflects back in mirror detail everything around it, 360 degrees, the trick is to find a spot that doesn't catch curving reflections of the telephone poles on the street or a fish-eye view of a concrete path. Move around the garden, setting up the pedestal and ball at different points and then stepping back to see the reflections from other spots in the garden—the path, for example, or the porch. Try places under tree branches, which provide interesting ceilings, or among tall flowers, as well as open places. Consider raising the pedestal on concrete pavers or jettisoning the pedestal and having the ball shine out from a dark mass of foliage. Carry the ball carefully; it's hand-blown glass and fragile.

Make a firm base for the pedestal. Rake the ground level, and moisten it if it's dry. Settle the pedestal firmly into the level wet soil.

Plant the aeoniums 6 inches from the pedestal, one alongside the other, in a cluster. Place the ball on the top of the pedestal.

Inexpensive
Easy
Location: Sun or shade

Tools
Rake
Hose or watering can
Planting trowel

Ingredients
Gazing ball, silver, large; in a bright garden, consider the less-reflective colors, such as dark blue, purple, or red
Pedestal, with hollow top or bowl to support stem of ball, 2½ feet tall or to suit garden (see text)
2 aeoniums or, in a cold-winter climate, houseleek (*Sempervivum* spp.)

Maintenance
Water plants regularly until established, then less frequently
Clean ball with damp cloth occasionally, to keep it bright

AQUATIC PLANT SOURCES

Your local general nursery probably sells a few water plants and may have the varieties best suited to the local climate. The companies listed here are water gardening specialists; they have aquatic nurseries open to the public and will send you a catalog for ordering plants and other supplies by mail.

Crystal Palace Perennials
12029 Wicker Avenue
Cedarlake, IN 46303
Tel: (219) 374-9419
Fax: (219) 374-9052
E-mail: gspeichert@aol.com
Retail nursery, free catalog, mail order

Hughes Water Gardens
25289 SW Stafford Road
Tualatin, OR 97062
Tel: (503) 638-2077
Fax: (503) 638-9035
E-mail: eamonn@teleport.com
Web site: http://www.watergardens.com
Retail nursery, free catalog, mail order

Lilypons Water Gardens
839 FM 1489
Brookshire, TX 77423-0188
Tel: (800) 723-7667
Fax: (713) 934-2000
Web site: http://www.lilypons.com
Retail nursery, free catalog, mail order

Lilypons Water Gardens
6800 Lilypons Road, P.O. Box 10
Buckeystown, MD 21717-0010
Tel: (800) 999-5459
Fax: (800) 964-7667
Web site: http://www.lilypons.com
Retail nursery, free catalog, mail order

Maryland Aquatic Nurseries
3427 North Furnace Road
Jarrettsville, MD 21084
Tel: (410) 557-7615
Fax: (410) 692-2837
E-mail: info@marylandaquatic.com
Web site: http://www.marylandaquatic.com
Retail nursery (Saturdays only), catalog (small charge), mail order

Perry's Water Gardens
1831 Leatherman Gap Road
Franklin, NC 28734
Tel: (704) 524-3264
Fax: (704) 369-2050
E-mail: perrywat@dnet.net
Retail nursery, catalog (small charge), mail order

Scherer Water Gardens
104 Waterside Road
Northport, NY 11768
Tel: (516) 261-7432
Fax: (516) 261-9325
Retail nursery, free catalog, mail order

Tilley's Nursery/The Water Works
111 East Fairmount Street
Coopersburg, PA 18036
Tel: (610) 282-4784
Fax: (610) 282-1262
E-mail: tilleys@itw.com
Retail nursery, free plant list, mail order

Waterford Gardens
74 East Allendale Road
Saddle River, NJ 07458
Tel: (201) 327-0721
Fax: (201) 327-0684
E-mail: splash@waterford-gardens.com
Web site: http://waterford-gardens.com
Retail nursery, catalog (small charge), mail order

BIBLIOGRAPHY

The following books have inspired and informed my writing on water and water gardens:

Adams, William Howard. *Roberto Burle Marx: The Unnatural Art of the Garden.* New York: Museum of Modern Art, 1991.

Allison, James. *Water in the Garden.* Blacksburg, Va.: Tetra Press, 1991.

Archer-Wills, Anthony. *The Water Gardener: A Complete Guide to Designing, Constructing, and Planting Water Features.* Hauppauge, N.Y.: Barron's Educational Series, 1993.

Church, Thomas D., Grace Hall, and Michael Laurie. *Gardens Are for People.* Berkeley and Los Angeles: University of California Press, 1995.

Claflin, Edward B. *Garden Pools and Fountains.* San Ramon, Calif.: Ortho Books, 1988.

Cooper, Guy, and Gordon Taylor. *English Water Gardens.* London: Weidenfeld & Nicholson, 1987.

——. *Paradise Transformed: The Private Garden for the Twenty-first Century.* New York: The Monacelli Press, 1996.

Crowe, Sylvia. *Garden Design.* Wappingers Falls, N.Y.: Antique Collectors' Club, 1994.

Eck, Joe. *Elements of Garden Design.* New York: Henry Holt & Co., 1995.

Hessayon, D. G. *The Rock and Water Garden Expert.* London: Transworld Publishers, 1995; distributed in the United States by Sterling Publishing, New York.

Hicks, David. *Garden Design.* London: Routledge & Kegan Paul, 1982.

Keen, Mary. *Decorate Your Garden: Affordable Ideas and Ornaments for Small Gardens.* London: Conran Octopus, 1993.

Moore, Charles W., William J. Mitchell, and William Turnbull Jr. *The Poetics of Gardens.* Cambridge, Mass.: MIT Press, 1988.

Nash, Helen. *The Pond Doctor: Planning and Maintaining a Healthy Water Garden.* New York: Sterling Publishing, 1995.

Page, Russell. *The Education of a Gardener.* New York: HarperCollins Publishers, 1994.

Paul, Anthony, and Yvonne Rees. *The Water Garden.* New York: Penguin Books, 1986.

Quick Guide: Ponds and Fountains. Upper Saddle River, N.J.: Creative Homeowner Press, 1994.

Stadelmann, Peter. *Water Gardens.* Hauppauge, N.Y.: Barron's Educational Series, 1992.

Stevens, David, and Ursula Buchan. *The Garden Book.* London: Conran Octopus, 1994.

Sunset Western Garden Book. Menlo Park, Calif.: Sunset Publishing, 1995.

Swindells, Philip, and David Mason. *The Complete Book of the Water Garden.* Woodstock, N.Y.: Overlook Press, 1990.

van Sweden, James. *Gardening with Water.* New York: Random House, 1995.

Wilkinson, Elizabeth, and Marjorie Henderson, eds. *Decorating Eden: A Comprehensive Sourcebook of Classic Garden Details.* San Francisco: Chronicle Books, 1992.

ACKNOWLEDGMENTS

I'm especially grateful to the team of Chronicle Books staff and freelancers who put this book together so beautifully: editors Bill LeBlond and Leslie Jonath, designer David Bullen, art director Michael Carabetta, copyeditor and dear friend Zipporah Collins, proofreader Ellen Klages, and assistant editor Sarah Putman.

Many landscape architects, garden designers, and technical experts shared their enthusiasms about water in the garden with me, especially Tom Chakas, Jack Chandler and Chris Moore, John Denning and Brigitte Micmacker at A New Leaf Gallery, Curtis Dennison at The Urban Farmer Store, George Little and David Lewis, Ron Lutsko, John MacRae, Suzanne Porter, and Roger Raiche.

Years ago when I saw Kent Gullickson and Joe Frankenfield's garden on a tour I dreamed of one day sitting in the sunshine by their pond. Thanks, Kent, for the memorable discussions there this year, and for reading the manuscript. Thanks also to Topher Delaney and Andy Cochran for imaginative talk, and to Sarah Hammond, Keeyla Meadows, Walt and Vicky McAllister, Sharon Osmond, Robin Parer, and Chris and Stephanie Tebbutt for special hospitality and friendship.

Matt and I are both greatly indebted to all those who opened their gardens to us for this book; thank you for your generosity—we were inspired by it, and by the time we spent watching your beautiful water gardens.

Finally, thanks to friends, especially Carol Henderson for encouragement, to David Goldberg and Pam Peirce and Jane Staw and colleagues for the same, and again to Bill LeBlond, who has helped so much to put this series in motion.

GARDEN CREDITS

Gardens and garden owners are listed in roman type; the landscape architect or designer, in italics.
Pages 1, 20, 27, 30: McAllister Water Gardens, Napa Valley; pages 2, 13, 59, 61, 67, 69: *Suzanne Porter;* pages 3, 41 (top): Potomac Waterworks; pages 7 (bottom), 28, 56 (fountain by Keeyla Meadows), 106: *Keeyla Meadows;* pages 8 (top), 100: Bloedel Reserve, Bainbridge Island, Washington; pages 8 (bottom), 85, 87: *Harland Hand;* pages 9 (top), 72: *Jack Chandler & Associates;* pages 9 (bottom), 33, 98, 99: *Sarah Hammond;* pages 11, 15, 16 (top), 54, 81, 83, 84: *Little and Lewis;* pages 12 (bottom), 19 (bottom): William and Sheri Slater; pages 14 ("Hexagonal Fountain," by Eric Norstad, "Large Mizubachi," by Michael Zimber, "Dark Oval," by Embree De Persiis), 16 (bottom, "Birdbath," by Dean Petaja), 17 (top, "Big Cup," by Patrick Fitzgerald; bottom, "Green Gobble," by Eric Norstad): A New Leaf Garden Gallery; pages 18, 50: *Sharon Osmond;* pages 19 (top), 52, 53: *Tom Chakas;* page 21: Carl and Sharon Anduri, *Matsutani and Associates;* pages 22, 24 (top): Western Hills Nursery and Garden; pages 23, 48, 49 (carved heads by Marcia Donahue): *Robin Parer, Geraniaceae;* pages 24 (bottom), 91, 93, 94: *Roger Raiche;* pages 25, 29, 42, 44, 88, 103, 104, 105: Jeff and Virginia Mitchell, Beija-flor Resort and Gardens, *Stephanie Kotin and Christopher Tebbutt, Land & Place;* pages 34, 41 (bottom): Rutherford Grill, Napa Valley, *Arnold Koenig, ASLA;* pages 36, 78: *Douglas Bayley, Landscape Designer;* Gail and Ron Gester, *Stephanie Kotin and Christopher Tebbutt, Land & Place;* pages 62, 63: Tony Rienzi, fountain created and installed by *John Denning, Brigitte Micmacker, A New Leaf Garden Gallery;* pages 64, 66: Robert and Mary Logan, *Susan Van Atta, ASLA;* pages 70, 111, 112: *John McRae;* pages 75, 77: Marjory Harris, *Harland Hand;* pages 95, 97: *Lutsko Associates, Landscape;* pages 108, 110: Barbara and Elliott Wolfe, *Delaney, Cochran, and Castillo.*

INDEX